how to collect
paper money

how to collect paper money

Colin Narbeth

Arthur Barker Limited

5 Winsley Street London W 1

Acknowledgements

The author wishes to record the valuable
assistance given him by Yasha Beresiner,
editor of the International Banknote Society
magazine, in checking and indexing this
book.

ISBN 0 213 00177 2
Printed in Great Britain by
C. Tinling & Co. Ltd, Prescot and London

contents

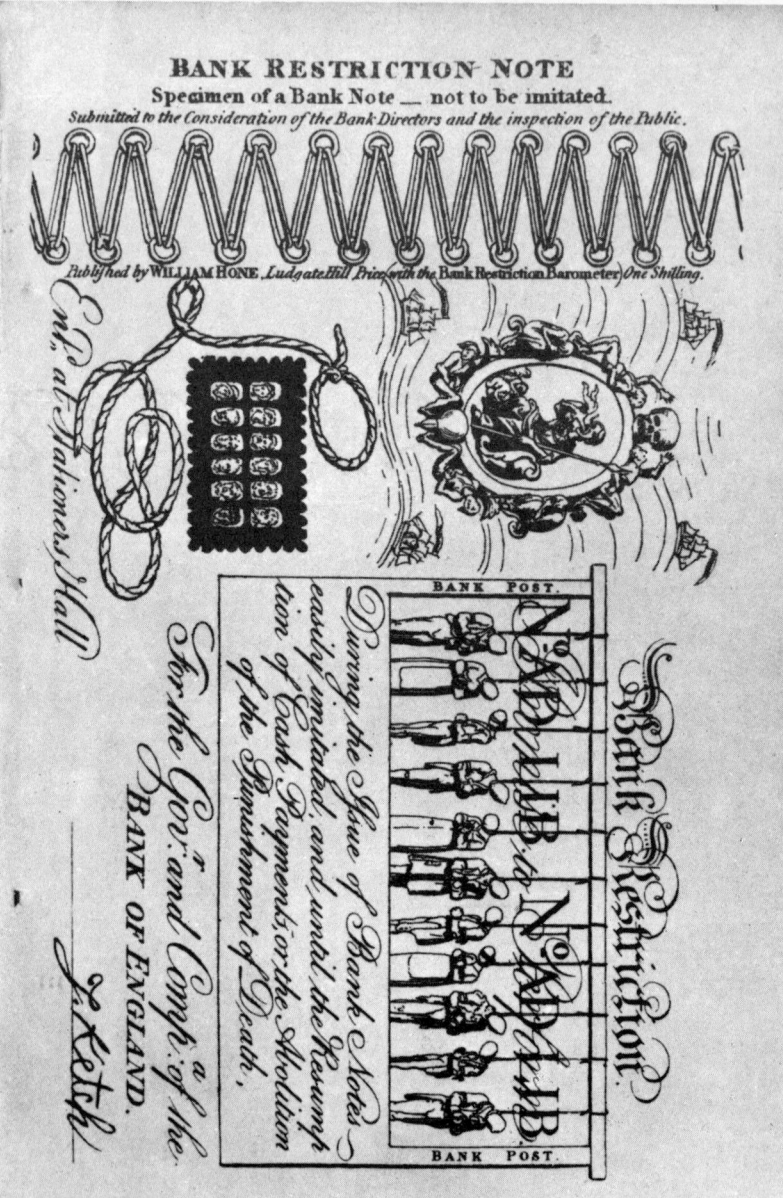

The anti-hanging note of George Cruikshank. When this note was sold on the streets the Lord Mayor of London had to send police to clear the crowds

1 introduction

Collecting paper money of the world is a hobby that, by and large, has been neglected for many years. But early in the 1900s a few serious collectors began to catalogue and study the various issues. At the time of World War I there was a sudden interest in paper money by German collectors who were flooded with *Notgeld* – emergency issues by every town and village in the nation. The strong tendency of officials to exploit the situation and issue set after set for the sole purpose of attracting collectors caused a loss of interest in them. Even so, today, *Notgeld* are no longer so easy to obtain and prices are rising.

From the 1930s the hobby began growing steadily with scholars giving attention to the subject – like Dr Arnold Keller who, in a period of twenty years, catalogued all German notes and many others as well.

After World War II paper money, as a hobby, was here to stay and growing steadily in popularity. Many collectors were put off the idea of collecting paper money because they believed that it was very expensive – a natural reaction when British paper money is almost invariably for high denominations and is often valid, if not legal tender. In reality it was possible to buy extremely rare items of paper money at prices very much less than one would have to pay for a coin of the same rarity. Lack of knowledge on the part of vendors often allowed collectors to purchase great rarities for a few shillings.

Only ten years ago it was possible to buy early Ming notes from

China for between £30 and £50. Today Ming notes are rapidly approaching the £400 mark and, in view of their extreme rarity and age, it is not surprising. We now know that even in the days of the French Revolution there were a few people who took an interest in paper issues, and a printed sheet, in colour, has been found which illustrates the majority of the Revolutionary notes and which was a contemporary printing. Generally, however, the early history of a nation's paper money is obscure and the collector who enjoys research will find plenty of scope.

Not only old notes need research. Many modern issues are almost unknown. Last year several new paper money items turned up that had been issued as real emergency money in certain prisoner-of-war camps of the last war. The possibility of a new find is greater than in any other hobby and adds to the excitement and attraction of the hobby.

Present trends indicate that paper money collecting may well become one of the major collecting hobbies in the world. There are a number of reasons why paper money collecting, once a collector is introduced to it, is taking precedence over other hobbies.

For one thing paper money was a substitute for coin only in times of emergency for hundreds of years. The people invariably preferred to have gold and silver and thus we find that the early paper money usually refers to great historic occasions when a nation faced an emergency. It will be seen that these items are therefore a part of history. In many cases they are the only historic reminders of certain events available to collectors. For example a number of sieges saw the issue of paper money but no coins at all. The French Revolution has left behind it a few coins but a flood of paper money which ably demonstrates the fortunes of the nation's economy.

Because people preferred metal coinage the issuers of early paper money went to considerable trouble to obtain the trust of the people. To do this they often had famous people hand-signing the notes. Early American paper money produced by the colonialists can be found with signatures of many famous men whose names also appear on the Declaration of Independence etc.

At the time of the siege of Khartoum, General 'Chinese' Gordon hand-signed a number of £50 notes and these were readily

Notgeld issued by towns and cities. Many thousands were issued

Khartoum Siege Note, handsigned by General Gordon

accepted in lieu of coin simply because they bore his personal signature.

Many insurgents had no means of producing metal coins and their fortunes hung around issues of paper money. Where they failed, the paper money is the only memento left of the occasion. The 1794 war of independence in Poland saw an issue of notes by the insurgents. The war failed and occasionally these notes turn up in near uncirculated condition. They are all that is left of the war from a collecting point of view.

As paper money came more and more to the front and coins were relegated to 'small change', the backing of the paper issues was often suspect. To overcome this the issuers would go to extremes to produce attractive, colourful, issues. The added difficulty of having to combat forgery made it necessary for governments to employ the very finest engravers and artists that they could obtain. The result is that a great proportion of paper money throughout the world is the product of the best artistic ability of the time.

The artists had a larger area to work in than they had on

Printer's specimen of Chartered Bank of India, Australia and China

postage stamps so the results were, artistically, preferable. The collector can produce a miniature art gallery through banknotes and it often happens that the banknote designs are miniatures of very famous paintings, or people.

Perhaps another great advantage which paper money enjoys over other collecting hobbies is that it has from the very start been protected by more laws than any other item. The danger of forgery was always such that every possible step was taken to stop people even imitating banknotes.

Until the last few years paper money was considered far too important to a nation's economy to produce 'special' issues. But in 1967 Canada issued what might be termed a commemorative banknote on the occasion of the nation's Centennial.

It is probable that many more countries will follow suit. The average life of paper in circulation is very short and, in some quarters, it is thought that a frequent change of design might act as a useful deterrent to forgers.

Naturally those countries whose issues of paper money are valid for all time (for example Great Britain, United States) are

11

expensive. The collector has to pay the face value of the note as well as its collector's rarity value. But this problem looks like being solved for future generations of collectors.

A number of organisations concerned with the production of paper money are examining the possibilities of producing 'Specimen' notes for collectors with the approval of the governments concerned. This can mean that a collector can purchase a £100 note of a foreign nation at very much less than face value. There is no question of the collector being 'taken for a ride' as he sometimes is with cancelled-to-order stamps which are deliberately made to look like genuinely used postage stamps. In this case the notes are clearly marked that they are 'Specimen' notes, and that therefore they are not currency. To the legions of collectors who would never be able to afford the price of high-denomination notes the Specimen issues would provide an example of the note design and quality.

Such specimen notes are not to be confused with the printers' specimen issues which are produced in small numbers basically for a particular reason, or with die-proofs, many of which are worth very much more to collectors than the actual banknotes.

Another great advantage of paper money is that it caters for all types of collector. Issues dating back to the Ming dynasty of China will satisfy those interested in ancient material. The idea that paper money is something modern is quite wrong. Paper money was circulating in China as early as 650 AD, according to some authorities, and was established by 800 AD.

One-country collectors will find many nations which will occupy their collecting interest for a lifetime. Notes can be collected for their historic association with events, for the artistic design, or even thematically.

Some of the important theme collections which have been formed include medicine on paper money and beehives on paper money. A great field for 'themes' is the *Notgeld* of Germany which covers so many subjects that almost any theme can be illustrated.

Some collectors try and get as many different denominations as possible and this can involve an enormous collection, including paper money for five halfpennies and odd denominations like that.

Among the more popular specialist fields for collecting is military currency. In World War II many countries issued quantities of military money. Add to that the invasion notes, prisoner-of-war notes and partisan issues and the collector has a wide field which can tell the story of the war.

Housing a collection does not present any great difficulties. An advantage over stamps and coins is that paper money can lend itself to being framed and put on a wall. An uncut sheet of banknotes can look very attractive, as can some of the giant Russian notes of the Tsarist period.

For those to whom expense is not a consideration special glass-framed cabinets with pull-out display frames can be made. These can look extremely attractive and can show both sides of a note. But, of course, they are very expensive and the majority of collectors would rather spend that sort of money on obtaining examples of paper money than on housing them.

Most collectors settle for the more conventional methods of display such as ordinary loose-leaf stamp albums. Photo-corners, hawid strips, etc., can be used to mount the notes. Also a number of special albums have been produced, notably by Stanley Gibbons Ltd, for the specific purpose of housing paper money.

An immediate reaction to mounting notes in ordinary stamp albums is that only one side of the note can be seen. This is very true but the new collector quickly finds that the vast majority of old notes are only printed on one side of the note anyway. And that among the modern notes most carry an identical design on one side so the collector only needs to duplicate one note in a set to show that side.

The special banknote albums allow both sides of a note to be seen, and insert leaves permit the collection to be 'written up'. Collectors should always be careful when housing notes in plastic pockets as these contain oil in order to make them supple. There is a possibility that the oil will cause a diffusion of fugitive inks, over a long period of time. To avoid this the collector should make sure that every now and then he examines the notes and takes them out of the pockets to allow air to circulate.

One of the major problems facing new collectors is that of condition. Whereas with coins there are established 'conditions' this is not so with paper money, though firms like Stanley Gibbons are trying to establish a system which can be universally accepted.

The equivalent of FDC (*fleur de coin*) in paper money is variously described as *Crisp, New, Mint, Uncirculated*. The numismatic definition *Extremely Fine* (EF) is used to denote that the note is nearly in this condition but has circulated very slightly, perhaps only to the extent of having a folding crease or a pin-hole or two. The original crispness, however, is still evident in the note.

The condition *Very Fine* (VF) indicates that the note has circulated to a greater degree, has collected one or two folds etc., but is still in clean condition and presents an attractive appearance.

Fine, as with the numismatic definition, describes a piece of paper money that has been well circulated and may have a small tear or two, has been folded and perhaps has a few stains but nevertheless, overall, retains an attractive appearance.

Very Good means that the note has circulated to an extent where the pleasing appearance has been destroyed. To a collector this means that the note is not worth including in his collection unless it is either very rare or very old. It happens that some notes, as the Portuguese notes of the War of the Two Brothers, circulated for as much as thirty years and were given 'official repairs' by the banks of issue. It would therefore be most unlikely that such a note would turn up in any condition but VG and its value would not be affected by such a low condition. As paper money was not collected at all in the early days, all paper money circulated unless it was accidentally saved for posterity. Therefore collectors will readily accept old notes in almost any condition, the age and historic importance taking precedence over condition. Exceptions to this are the issues of the French Revolution and certain early issues of Paraguay etc. Here the notes were issued in such quantities and replaced so frequently that collectors can expect them to turn up in reasonably good, if not crisp, condition. In the case of Paraguay an early issue of notes is often found in VF condition and above for the simple reason that a war of annihilation wiped out three-quarters of the population and there was more paper money than people to spend it!

As a general rule collectors do not expect the perfection of condition that a numismatist expects, or aims at. Paper money deteriorates very quickly in circulation, unlike coins, and many of the early issues are unknown in crisp condition. With modern notes, naturally, the collector looks for crisp condition because they are still obtainable. Even so, the normal issues of Great Britain of twenty years ago are scarce in crisp condition and in VF condition fetch high prices.

With extremely dirty notes or very badly creased notes it is possible to increase their attractiveness by washing them and pressing them between heavy books, without causing any damage to the note. But as a general rule it is better to leave the item in its original state and only to clean it if its appearance is so dirty as to be unsightly in a collection.

Even a small collection of paper money can be instructive educationally, can be made to unravel history and in many instances can actually corroborate historical events. Students of a nation's economy find the paper money issues a major 'give-away' to what really happened. Inflation can be traced and experiments in paper money issues studied advantageously. Few hobbies can offer the excitement of the 'new finds' still available in the paper money field, or the magnitude of different types of collection that can be formed. From a purely investment angle paper money is likely to be one of the great bets of the future. As the hobby spreads early paper money is going to treble in value quickly once its true scarcity and historic importance is fully appreciated.

2 british paper money

The forerunner of paper money – leather – has been claimed by some numismatists to have been issued in Britain during the reign of King Eadgar, the great-grandson of King Alfred the Great. It is highly unlikely that such an issue ever existed in fact and, indeed, one of the British Museum's top experts on Anglo-Saxon numismatics, Mr R. H. M. Dolley, made a detailed study of the evidence and concluded that no serious case can be made out for the issue.

In short, the existence of such leather money relies on a verse in the *Comedy of the Wits* (an early masterpiece by the seventeenth century English playwright, Sir William D'Avenant, 1606–1668) which reads:

> Why this was such a firk of piety
> I ne'er heard of: bury her gold with her;
> 'Tis strange her old shoes were not interr'd too,
> For fear the days of Edgar should return
> When they coin'd leather.

No supporting evidence has ever emerged. There is a probability, however, that leather money was used in the Tudor period. Also a detailed description exists for a leather issue by Edward I for Wales – though none has ever come to light.

The earliest known piece of paper money in Britain appears to be a Military Payment Certificate issued on 14 March 1635. It is a pay warrant to Sir Francis Godolphin, Commander of the Garrison of the Isle of Shelley off the coast of Cornwall. It is signed by Francis, Baron Cottingham, Lord Treasurer of England and reads:

'After my harty commendacions as the weal, Francis Godolphin known to his Majesties Receiver General of the Counties of Devon and Cornwall, hath informed me that formerly he hath a respite of the Some of Four Hundred Pounds for and twords the payment of himself and his soldiers at Captains of The Garrison of the Isle of Schilley. These are therefore to require you to respite upon his attempt [meaning 'request'] now in passing the said some of Four Hundred Pounds until [by] Michaelmas come next. And for so doing, THIS SHALL BE YOUR WARRANT.

Your loving friend,
Francis Cottingham

14th March 1635
To my loving friend,
Richard Kinsman Esq.,
His Majesties Auditor
of the said Counties'

The fathers of the banking world in Britain were the goldsmiths. It must be remembered that in the days of the goldsmith bankers the current methods of transacting business did not exist. Payments were more often than not made in bullion. Merchants found it difficult to safely store bullion and the goldsmiths' vaults were convenient. Naturally the goldsmith would issue a receipt and gradually the practice grew up of using these receipts to transact business. They represented actual gold and silver and were freely accepted from merchant to merchant.

Almost as a natural follow-on the goldsmiths began issuing cash notes to depositors and for a long time the common practice was to endorse the notes with the amounts paid on them, thus gradually reducing the value of the note.

It became convenient for goldsmiths to issue notes of fixed amounts so that such a multitude of endorsements were not necessary and for some time these were made in denominations of £5, £10, or £100 to suit the personal requirements of the customer. All these notes were made out by hand until about 1735 when printing was used.

Just when the goldsmith notes started is not known. But it is likely that the 'banking power' moved over to the goldsmiths in the reign of Charles I, for at that time it was the practice of many merchants to deposit their valuables in the Tower of London for safe-keeping. Charles I anticipated the Civil War's financial requirements by confiscating the treasure in the Tower. This lost him the confidence of the merchants who turned to the goldsmiths for safe-keeping.

It follows that most of the original London bankers were goldsmiths. One of the oldest banks known, that of Child and Company, can trace its history to the reign of Queen Elizabeth I. Of the twenty banks which joined to form Barclays Bank, the one bearing the familiar name – Barclay, Bevan, Tritton, Ransom, Bouverie and Co. (London and Brighton) – traces its own history to the goldsmith John Freame of Lombard Street. He founded the Bank of Freame and Gould well prior to the Bank of England (1694), at the sign of the Three Anchors. It was not until 1728 that John Freame bought premises in Lombard Street known as the Black Spread Eagle – a sign still used by Barclays Bank. An interesting notice appears in the London Gazette of 7 December 1702 in which John Freame offered a reward for one of his cash notes which had been lost.

In the early days there were no restrictions on the issue of paper money and in consequence many groups of people got together and formed banks. By 1793 there were something like 400 note-issuing banks in Britain – and it must be remembered that the population of Britain was much smaller than it is now! There was a general collapse of credit in that year and just over a third of those banks collapsed, causing much misery to many people.

In 1797 even the Bank of England was forced to suspend special payments and it is to be noted that during the period 1797–1821 every bank in Europe suspended payments.

Sir Robert Peel's Bank Charter Act of 1844 was the first to bring real control over note-issuing banks and from that time onwards lists of banks and their returns appeared in the *Bankers' Almanack*. No bank was allowed to issue notes within a 65-mile range of London so that the Bank of England enjoyed a complete monopoly in that area. The 1844 Act limited the

18

A British Provincial note of 1848

number of note-issuing banks to under 300 and these gradually ceased to function until in 1921 the last surviving bank to issue its own notes, Fox, Fowler and Co., amalgamated into Lloyds Bank.

Collectors will often find that the old provincial banknotes have printed words on the backs to indicate that they had been exhibited at bankruptcy proceedings. It is very difficult for collectors to value these old notes and generally they are divided into large circulation banks, small circulation banks and those which are still honoured because the banks merged with practising bankers.

There are a number of interesting notes which appeared at this time.

The great Utopian, Robert Owen (1771–1858), formulated his ideas amid the revolutionary sentiments which began to spread as a result of unemployment, low wages and higher taxes. He started a journal, *Crisis,* in 1832 which he used to express his ideas of co-operation and exchange bazaars.

He felt that real economic justice could not exist if workers

A Robert Owen note for one-hour. An early socialist Owen believed that all men should work according to their ability and be paid the same – that is by the number of hours they worked

were paid with money which fluctuated in value. He therefore introduced his own solution, special paper money with denominations in hours of work, which could be exchanged for goods.

He opened the London Exchange Bazaar in 1832. It accepted commodities from anyone, pricing being done by valuers who determined the value of the raw material and the labour time necessary for its production. The producer was given paper notes for 'labour hours'. The notes were issued on thick paper in units of 1, 2, 5, 10, 20, 50, 80, and 100 hours. They bore the inscription: 'The Exchange Bank operates on the principle of Justice. The value of labour amounts to sixpence an hour. Present to the bearer on demand goods to the value of...hours'. Owen signed all the notes.

Although the bazaar enjoyed an initial success, and even private traders at first accepted the notes, it was doomed to failure. Some goods were more popular than others and the situation arose in which a purchaser found that all the things that were popular had gone and he was left with a choice of things he did not want. He would then try to change his note with private tradesmen, and this led to discounts and depreciation. In 1834 the bazaar had to close and Robert Owen had to cover a deficit of more than £2000.

George Cruikshank made a satirical note in his support against the numerous hangings for forgery. The note has skulls round the figure of Britannia and is signed by 'Jack Ketch' the hangman, for in the early 1800s the mere possession of a forged Bank of England note could lead to the hangman's rope. In a space of thirteen years over 200 people were hanged for the offence while many hundreds were convicted and imprisoned or deported. Things came to a head in 1819 when a man was hanged for imitating a bank note and the Society of Arts issued a report 'relative to the mode of preventing the forging of bank notes'.

The report, apart from an unjustified optimism in the immunity of the stereotyping process from imitation, is of great interest. The Committee pressed for the immediate adoption of a complicated design, engraved for intaglio printing by one of the best artists of the day. The report stated: 'There are not less than 10,000 persons in the country who are able to engrave successful imitations of Bank of England Notes – and nine-tenths of these are in needy, and many of them in distressed, circumstances'. The designs, it said, should be so intricate that they were no longer 'the commonplace work of inferior writing engravers but became masterpieces of the best engravers and would pass beyond the scope of common forgery'.

Naturally this led to the Banks being given all sorts of suggestions from many artists. None of the ideas was used but some of the designs can still be found by collectors.

Perhaps one of the most amusing forgeries of notes was that of a French prisoner of war imprisoned in Edinburgh during the Napoleonic Wars. He even sent out from the prison orders to buy the right type of paper he needed – and then he proceeded to produce, rather well, the current notes in use in the City.

Few forgeries were superior enough to fool anyone for long. Although some of them have a collector's interest, it is against the law of Great Britain to possess forged banknotes. However, collectors in other countries regard the most historically important forgery to be that of the Bank of England notes made by the Germans in World War II. There is no doubt that many of these defy identification by collectors, although Bank of England tellers are able to spot the forgeries in a moment.

the big forgery

Their story is worth relating. Nine million forged notes with a face value of around 140 million pounds is the conservative estimate of the amount of forged paper money produced by the Germans during World War II with the intention of disrupting the British economy.

That the project failed was, strangely enough, nothing to do with the quality of the notes, which were quite capable of fooling the world in general, but simply because, as Major Kruger put it: 'If you don't slow down I will be sent to the Russian front and you will all be shot'.

Major Kruger was in charge of Operation Bernhard (as the scheme was called) and employed more than a hundred convicted forgers, having found the printers at the Reichsbank too Prussian in their outlook.

Overall the operation was under Heinrich Himmler and was known as Office 6–F–4. It was set up in the Block 19 compound at Oranienburg. Guarded by hand-picked men of the Deathshead Division, the forgers were permitted anything they wanted by way of machinery.

The first notes off the presses were quietly sent to German representatives in Turkey, Spain, Switzerland and other neutral countries. They were, in most cases, accepted without trouble. One agent captured at Edinburgh had a suitcase full of forged fivers, and Germany began to pay off its informers in forged currency. Indeed, the most famous spy of the war, Cicero, who thought he was the highest-paid spy ever when he received £300,000 for the secrets he stole from the British Ambassador's safe at Ankara, was paid in forged money.

The notes were sorted into three grades. The best were for circulating in neutral countries (some are known to have gone through neutral countries to Britain and then back again!). Grade

Two were for paying collaborators (they could fool everyone except the Bank of England), and Grade Three were stored ready for dropping by plane over England. The British population, the Germans felt with some justification, would welcome the delivery. The camp reached a production figure of 50,000 a month.

To postpone his commitment to the Russian front the Major, who seems to have had a very glib tongue, persuaded the authorities that he should also forge US dollars and ruin their economy at the same time. When Allied advances made the whole scheme useless he still managed to keep away from the Russian Front by arguing the importance of supplying forged money etc. to senior Germans in the event of a surrender.

The British first realised the enormity of the programme when a German officer surrendered a convoy containing 21 million pounds of English notes. Questioned closely, the officer led investigators to Redl Zipf where in a honeycombed redoubt the machinery was found. The plates have never been found. Scotland Yard sent experts and the investigation was given top priority along with tracking down leading Nazis.

It was found that the forgers had been sent to Ebensee for extermination. But the commandant had let them go because Allied troops were in the area. Some forty of the ordinary forgers were traced before they caught the important forger.

Oskar Skala was innocuously serving beer near Pilsen when secret agents burst into the café. The Allies had caught the chief book-keeper of the whole operation.

Although the Allies tried hard to catch Major Kruger their search ended at the beginning of the tracks of his sports car. Witnesses reported that he had arrived at the compound in the sports car plus a beautiful blonde and boxes full of genuine notes. He had issued orders that the compound was to be destroyed along with the inmates, regretting that he was unable to supervise the affair because Himmler wanted him urgently. And that was the last time Major Kruger was seen or heard of.

Nearly forty million of the notes were hidden in coffin-sized boxes in the River Enns and Lake Toplitz – but some of the boxes broke open and Allied soldiers went swimming in winter until the attraction was discovered.

24

the bank of england

Today the Bank of England is the pivot of the British economy, yet its foundation was almost hidden in the Bill which made it possible. As Lord Macaulay, one of England's greatest historians, put it:

> 'It was ... not easy to guess that a Bill which purported only to impose a new duty on tonnage for the benefit of such persons as should advance money towards carrying on the war, was really a Bill creating the greatest commercial institution that the world has ever seen.'

A Scotsman, William Paterson, was behind the idea of the Bill 'for granting to Their Majesties several Rates and Duties upon Tonnage of Ships and Vessels and upon Beer, Ale and other Liquors; for securing certain Recompenses and Advantages in the said Act mentioned to such Persons as shall Voluntarily Advance the sum of Fifteen hundred thousand pounds towards carrying on the War against France'.

The recompenses and advantages were that they could raise a loan of £1,200,000 and create 'The Governor and Company of the Bank of England' with the right to issue notes. The capital was to be lent to the Crown at 8 per cent interest.

The wealthy Whig merchants quickly subscribed, and within four days over £900,000 had been raised. The King subscribed £10,000 through the Treasury.

John Evelyn's diary entry for 1 July 1694 reads:

> 'The first greate Bank for a fund of money being now established by Act of Parliament was fill'd and compleated to the sum of £120,000 [he meant £1,200,000] put under the government of the most able and wealthy citizens of London. All who adventur'd any sum had 4 per cent so long as it lay in the Bank, and had power either to take it out at pleasure or transfer it.'

The first governor was Sir John Houblon and the first Deputy Governor Michael Godfrey, both grocers. Sir John was also the Lord Mayor of London and Master of the Grocers Company.

In the beginning there were doubts among all parties in Parliament – King William III had given strong backing to the idea and it was felt that he might try and borrow direct from the Bank without sanction from Parliament. This was avoided by a special clause. It was William Pitt who many years later was able to avoid the clause and nearly ruin the Bank.

The Bank commenced business in the Hall of the Ancient Livery Company of Grocers and was known as 'Ye Bank in ye Poultry'.

In 1734 it moved to Threadneedle Street (the name then being Three Needles Street).

The most perilous moment in the Bank's history was the Gordon Riots when, on 6 June 1780, Lord George Gordon headed a vast mob which raided the Newgate Prison and then attacked the Bank of England. Only the timely intervention of the military saved the Bank, and from that date onwards the Brigade of Guards has furnished a Bank Guard.

The first issue of the Bank was 'running cash notes' written by hand on paper purchased from an ordinary stationer. These notes could be 'part-paid' by having appropriate endorsements made on them. The large custom the stationer attracted soon caused the Bank of England to find another source of supply.

Notes appeared on marbled paper. In the eighteenth century the Britannia design was moved from the centre to the left-hand side, but otherwise there was little change in the overall design.

At first the name of the payee was inserted by hand but this was later changed to the name of a Bank of England staff man. The first of these were Edward Clarke and John Miller. Notes bearing the names of Henry Hase or Abraham Newland, Chief Cashiers from 1798 to 1826, are the first notes which collectors have a reasonable chance of obtaining. £1 notes of this period have a value of about £150.

Many of the notes had the amount also written in by hand. The first printed notes issued in 1695 had been for £10, £20, £30, £40, £50, and £100. After forgery the amount was written in by hand until 1725 when printed denominations were used again and notes were issued for £20, £30, £40, £50, £60, £70, £80, £90, £100, £200, £300, £400, £500, and £1,000.

New denominations of £10 and £15 came out in 1795 followed by a £25 note in 1765.

It was not until 1793 that the Bank of England issued £5, £2, and £1 notes. Some notes are found with two halves taped

together. This is because of the practice of cutting the note in half
and sending one half first to avoid robbery.

modern issues

Modern Bank of England notes may be said to start with the
twentieth century. At the turn of the century £5 notes and above
were signed by H. G. Bowen and were still in the nineteenth-
century style. These were followed by notes signed by J. G.
Nairne, from 1902 to 1918, and the Bank of England clearly
considered re-introducing the £1 note as a specimen £1 was
produced in 1914. It never came to fruition, no doubt because of
the introduction of Treasury notes (see p. 29).

The Chief Cashier from 1918 to 1925 was E. M. Harvey and
during his period of office only white notes of £5 and over were
issued. The next Chief Cashier, C. P. Mahon, saw the re-
introduction of £1 and 10s. notes, in 1928, by the Bank of
England.

Collectors seeking these low denominations will find the following major types:

Pound notes:

A. Newlands	1797	handsigned
A. Newlands	1798	printed sign
A. Newlands	1801	date on right hand side
H. Hase	1807	countersigned
H. Hase	1808	Uncountersigned
H. Hase	1809	Caslon serial numbers
H. Hase	1810–21	Date centred
H. Hase	1825	Re-dated 1825 on 1821 notes
C. P. Mahon	1928	Green
B. G. Catterns	1929–34	Green
K. O. Peppiatt	1934–40	Green
K. O. Peppiatt	1940	Light blue with metal strip
K. O. Peppiatt	1940	Dark blue
K. O. Peppiatt	1948	Green (extra serial letter)
K. O. Peppiatt	1948	Green with strip
P. S. Beale	1949–55	Green with strip
L. K. O'Brien	1955–60	Green with strip
L. K. O'Brien	1960–2	Green, small size notes

One of the unissued Treasury notes prepared for use during the 1914–18 war

J. Q. Hollom	1962–6	Small size green
J. S. Fforde	1966–70	Small size green
J. Page	1970–	Small size green

Ten shilling notes:

C. P. Mahon	1928	Brown
B. G. Catterns	1929–34	Brown
K. O. Peppiatt	1934–40	Brown
K. O. Peppiatt	1940	Mauve with strip
K. O. Peppiatt	1948	Brown with strip
P. S. Beale	1949–55	Brown with strip
L. K. O'Brien	1955–60	Brown with strip
L. K. O'Brien	1961	Brown, small size
J. Q. Hollom	1962–66	Brown, small size
J. S. Fforde	1966–70	Brown, small size
	1970	Withdrawn

In 1957 there was a radical change made in the British £5 notes which were then issued in a new blue design known as the lion and key issue. The following year they underwent a minor change when the £5 symbol was printed in white instead of black. Yet another change was to take place with the introduction of the Britannia reverse in 1963.

During World War I, Treasury notes for 5s. and 2s. 6d. had been produced and, with the advent of World War II, the Bank of England prepared issues of the 5s. and 2s. 6d. notes but these were never needed and stocks were destroyed.

In 1964 the £10 note was re-introduced, and 1970 saw the re-introduction of the £20 which had been withdrawn in 1943. Shortly after that the whole range of notes was changed.

treasury notes

Austria–Hungary was looking for trouble with Serbia in the summer of 1914 and, when a Bosnian student, Gavrile Princip, shot dead the Archduke Franz Ferdinand of Austria, that was excuse enough. An ultimatum was sent in such wording that war became inevitable. Within two weeks of the assassination the London branch of the Dresdner Bank started selling off securities, a situation quickly noticed by its customers: an international crisis was on hand.

The public demand grew and intensified as Austro–Hungarian troops crossed into Serbia with a declaration of war. Even more ineffectual than they had been against the Italians, they were soon driven back and Serbian troops occupied part of Hungary. This was a position Germany could not tolerate and its troops moved to assist the Austrians, and the world was soon at war.

The effect on finance was immediate. Banks called in their money from the bill-brokers and this caused a large drain on the Bank of England. The Bank Rate went up to 8 per cent, the London Stock Exchange closed and the mid-August Settling Day was postponed.

The government hastily intervened in the gathering crisis and suspended the Bank Charter Act of 1844 so that the Bank was not obliged to pay out in gold. On 1 August the Bank Rate was 10 per cent.

England declared war on 4 August 1914 and the Bank had only £9 million of gold reserve. The Fiduciary Issue was £18,450,000 but against all this England had very favourable trade-balances of £207,000,000 and £4,000,000,000 in foreign and colonial securities.

The Chancellor of the Exchequer, Mr Lloyd George, was faced with the problem of a possible shortage of money. Paper money had to be printed quickly and in order to do this without arousing public fear, the Chancellor used the expedient of prolonging the August Bank Holiday by three whole days. This gave the printing presses breathing time.

At the same time, on 5 August, the government quickly passed the Currency and Bank Notes Act 1914, allowing the Treasury to print its own notes. These were £1 black and 10s. red notes.

The last issue of Bradbury Treasury Notes

Warren Fisher ten shilling note

Although intended to be called Treasury Notes they were soon referred to as Bradburys because they were signed by the then Secretary of the Treasury, Sir John Bradbury, later to be made Lord Bradbury. Postal orders were also declared legal tender.

During the next six years a total of £300 million in Treasury notes was issued.

Small denomination notes were also prepared for use in World War II and are signed by the Chief Cashier Peppiatt. They were never issued

In the first three days of war the presses turned out Treasury notes on the only paper available, paper normally reserved for printing stamps and licences. It is interesting to note that 5s. and 2s. 6d. notes were also printed in case of a shortage of small coin but were never, in fact, issued. (Some of them have got into collectors' hands.)

The last issue of the notes had the inscription 'United Kingdom of Great Britain and Northern Ireland' as against the earlier wording 'United Kingdom of Great Britain and Ireland'.

Collectors classify these notes as follows:

1	Bradbury 1st issue	£1	7 August-October 1914	Black and white on stamp watermarked paper
2		10s.	14 August-January 1915	Red and White
3	Bradbury 2nd issue	£1	October 1914-February 1917	Black and white
4		10s.	January 1915-November 1918	Red and white
5	A variety can be found of both £1 and 10s.			
6	Bearing an overprint in Arabic. These were issued to British troops embarking for the invasion of the Dardanelles in 1915 and were intended to represent 120 and 60 Turkish piastres respectively, during the occupation. The campaign was unsuccessful and the notes had a short duration.			
7	Bradbury 3rd issue	£1	February 1917–1919	Green and Brown
8		10s.	November 1918–1919	Green Serial No. in Red
9				Serial No. in Black
10	Fisher 1st issue	£1	October 1919–1923	Continuous watermark
11		10s.	,, ,,	
12	Fisher 2nd issue	£1	1923	Square watermark
13		10s.	,, ,,	Word "No." before serial number deleted
14	Fisher 3rd issue	£1	1928 ,, ,,	G.B. and Northern Ireland
15		10s.		,, ,, ,,

3 british paper money, part 2

scotland

Scotland was not long in following England in introducing paper money. Within a few months of the founding of the Bank of England, the Bank of Scotland was established. An English merchant, John Holland, was instrumental in its establishment and a bank charter was granted by Act of Parliament in 1695. The first notes were issued in 1696 and consisted of £5 and higher denominations. It was not until 1704 that Scotland issued its first pound notes through the Bank of Scotland. Such notes carry the wording '£12' but equalled the English £1.

This bank, however, failed to take the precaution to renew its monopoly and after successfully trading for twenty-one years and renewing its charter to continue banking it failed to ask for the monopoly it had previously enjoyed. The result was that the Royal Bank of Scotland was created and issued its first notes in 1727. The Bank of Scotland protested vigorously that '... it is impracticable to support and carry on two Banking companies in one country: no nation did ever attempt it', but without success.

Both banks embarked on a policy of trying to force the other to close its doors. This was achieved by amassing large quantities of the other's notes and then suddenly presenting them for payment. If the Bank could not find the metal coin in sufficient quantity it would be obliged to close its doors temporarily – and lose the trust of the people. The Bank of Scotland was worried by these tactics to the extent that it issued 'option notes' which were to 'Pay to ...

Top Stornaway also produced beautifully engraved notes at this period with colour printing on the reverses

Bottom An East Lothian Bank note with an interesting history. The Chief Cashier, Borthwick, absconded with £21,000 and was never caught. At one stage he had laid plans to have a suspicious director stuffed in a puncheon of whisky and shipped to Russia. The bank failed

or bearer one pound sterling on demand, or in the option of the Directors one pound sixpence sterling at the end of six months after the day of the demand'.

The notes effectively ended the competition between the two banks but were made illegal in 1766 when, at the same time, banks in Scotland were prohibited from issuing notes of £1 and less.

Linen was a major Scottish trade and the Edinburgh Linen Co-Partnery successfully petitioned for a charter to form the British Linen Bank in 1747, though when they started it was simply to facilitate the company's shortage of capital. Promissory notes were issued for £5 and higher denominations and found a ready reception among the public. In 1750 the company issued £1 and 10s. notes and by 1760 the banking side of the British Linen Company was so profitable that the bulk of its business became banking. Many other banks sprang up, as in England, and a great many of them went bankrupt. But thirty-three important Scottish banks always honoured their notes and were finally absorbed into other banks and still have their note issues honoured today.

In recent years there were a number of note-issuing banks in Scotland but they amalgamated into four as follows:

1 The Royal Bank of Scotland incorporated
    the National Commercial Bank of Scotland,
    the National Bank of Scotland, and
    the Commercial Bank of Scotland
2 The British Linen Bank
3 The Bank of Scotland incorporated
    the Union Bank of Scotland and
    the Caledonian Bank
4 The Clydesdale Bank (previously known as the Clydesdale and North of Scotland Bank) incorporated
    the North of Scotland Bank and
    the Town and County Bank

Two of these, the Bank of Scotland and the British Linen Bank, completed their amalgamation in 1970, which left three note-issuing banks.

The twentieth-century issues of Scotland are the most colourful and attractive paper money of Great Britain and are very popular with collectors. Until about 1927 the notes were very large for small denominations, being five by six inches and giving a nearly square appearance. Notes bore two signatures, and normally one would be printed and the other handwritten. In 1927 smaller notes were used, bringing the Scottish issues more in line with those of the Bank of England, but the practice of hand-signing notes often continued until the 1930s, when the amount of notes needed for circulation made hand-signing impracticable.

The size of notes was again reduced in the 1960s and has recently been reduced again to conform to the Bank of England specifications.

Specialists have a formidable task with the magnetic ink markings (MIM) introduced in 1967. These were put on the backs of banknotes in such a way that each major bank could be identified from the coding.

Two important books exist for collectors of Scottish notes, but are both out of print and difficult to obtain. They are:
History of Banking in Scotland by A. W. Kerr, and *The One Pound Note* by William Graham (Edinburgh 1886).

channel islands

An essential part of any collection of paper money of Great Britain, the Channel Islands provide some very colourful and historically interesting notes. Guernsey first used £1 notes around 1808 when the Bank of Guernsey and the Brock and Le Mesurier opened. These are extremely rare because both banks ceased operations by 1811. A few years later in 1816 the States of Guernsey issued their own notes in £1 denominations and to the total value of £4,000 and these were redeemed in 1818. The purpose of the issue was to facilitate the building of the Torteval Church and Jerbourg Monument.

Other early issues of the States of Guernsey were:

1820	£1 notes	£4,500		
1826	£1 notes	£20,000	£5 notes	£10,000

Private banks began opening again in 1827. The Guernsey Banking Company was the largest of these with its notes widely

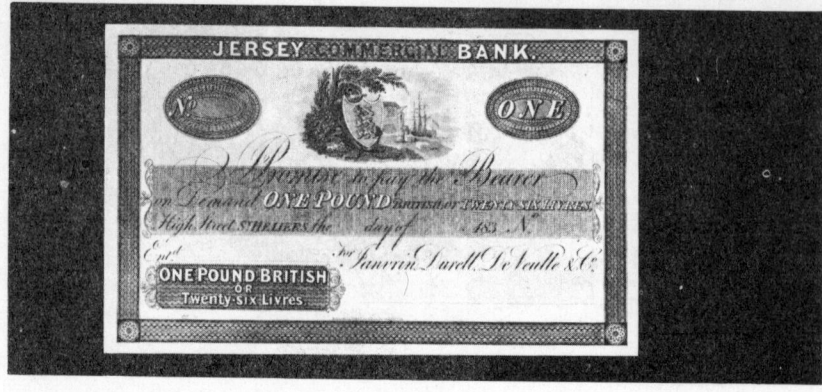

Private nineteenth-century note of Jersey

used in Alderney, St Malo and Cherbourg. The notes were printed by Perkins, Bacon Ltd, who printed the first adhesive postage stamps in 1840.

For a time the States agreed to limit its issue of notes in order to help the private banks, but by 1914 these agreements ceased and the States issued larger quantities and added low denominations of 5s. and 10s.

All notes issued by the States were hand-signed by the Treasurer until 1921, when a printed signature was used.

World War II saw an early occupation of the Channel Islands by the Germans. Coin was quickly hoarded and virtually disappeared. German occupation currency, as used on the Continent, was used as well as locally printed notes in denominations of 6d., 1s., 1s. 3d., 2s. 6d., and 5s. in Guernsey.

They came into circulation as follows:

2s. 6d. and 5s.	7 April 1941	
1s. 3d.	10 November 1941	
6d.	19 November 1941	
6d.	1 January 1942	(a new printing made on French banknote paper)
1s.	1942	Overprinted on the 1s. 3d. notes in red

Higher denominations were also produced. The 10s. and £1 were printed in 1943, without German authority and under the noses of the sentries in readiness for liberation. These notes, were released on Liberation Day, 9 May 1945, and the Channel Islands

An 1865 issue of the Guernsey Banking Company

received a special commendation from the Bank of England for being so quick to restore normal banking and note issues. A £5 note, the rarest of all Channel Islands notes, was also issued.

Of these notes only the £1 was pictorial, containing a design of St Peter Port harbour. All showed the coat of arms of Guernsey. Quantities printed are believed to be:

6d.	180,000	5s.	72,000
1s.	75,000	10s.	88,000
1s. 3d.	24,500	£1	172,000
2s. 6d.	164,000	£5	30,000

These figures are, however, misleading as many of the notes were taken by German soldiers as souvenirs and many more were destroyed or exchanged for German occupation notes. All the local issues are rare and the three top denominations are very rare. It is interesting to note that when the Allies re-occupied the Islands they honoured the German occupation notes and for a short time advertised in the local papers to exchange them at the rate of 2s. per Reichsmark.

British banknotes enjoy a wide circulation in Guernsey today alongside the present 10s., £1, and £5 States notes.

Alderney also had its own bank at one stage, as a £1 note is known from the Alderney Commercial Bank dated 1810.

Jersey was the first of the Channel Islands to open a bank. This was the Jersey Old Bank started by Hugh Godfray and Co., who were wine merchants. Various issues of £1 notes were made by this bank between 1797 and 1843. In 1887 it was incorporated into the Midland Bank, which would still honour its notes.

For a time, as in England, many people in Jersey decided to issue their own notes, and during the Napoleonic Wars Jersey had a wide range of low-denomination notes, most of which were not redeemed on presentation. This was effectively stopped when legislation was passed preventing the use of notes below the value of £1. Nevertheless by 1817 over one hundred note-issuing offices existed.

Some of the early notes of Jersey were issued in livre denominations. The States of Jersey as such do not appear to have issued notes until 1874 when a £1 note was issued by the Harbour Committee and redeemed by 1884.

World War II also caused a shortage of small money, and Jersey and Guernsey produced denominations such as 6d., 1s., 1s. 3d., 2s., 5s., 10s., £1.

Edmund Blampied, a well-known artist of the Islands, designed a set of five notes which was issued on 20 April 1942: 6d. with the words 'sixpence' interwoven as the design, 1s. (two people), 2s., 10s. (milkmaid and cows), £1 (seaweed gathering). An earlier 2s. note was issued on 31 May 1941.

Printing quantities were:

2s.	1941	50,000	2s.	1942	50,000
6d.	1942	840,000	10s.	,,	26,000
1s.	,,	200,000	£1	,,	11,000

Despite the low printings, the high-value denominations appear more often than do those of Guernsey.

The States of Jersey made an issue of notes in 1963 of 10s., £1, and £5 with the Annigoni portrait of the Queen.

british paper money values

With the sudden rise in popularity of old paper money there has developed a need for fair and proper valuation of notes. This extensive interest in notes is reflected throughout the world.

Prices of British paper money have moved up over the last decade but it is quite probable that many of them are going to more than double their present value in the near future.

One of the difficulties is that some notes have not been offered on the open market, and others so seldom that a true worth cannot be estimated. The goldsmiths, the fathers of banking, introduced their own notes which enjoyed extensive circulation. The value of those issued prior to the foundation of the Bank of England have been estimated at £100, and the probability is that they would fetch more in open market.

It is with the inception of the Bank of England in 1694 that the average collector comes into a range of notes within his reach, except for the hand-written issues.

Early issues are all scarce and in 1797 the Revolutionary and Napoleonic Wars caused the Bank of England to suspend specie payment. This continued until 1816 when a partial redemption was attempted and then postponed until 1821, when the Bank once again redeemed its issues – but at a discount!

Collectors assess the provincial and private banknotes which come from bankrupt firms (see page 20) only in a very general way because of the lack of knowledge about them. Some are virtually unique, but because little is known about them they still sell at prices charged for more common issues.

Since they have no valid face value the denomination on the note has little effect on the collectors' value. When the banking confusion was finally put in order by the Bank Charter Act of 1844 lists were compiled (and can be found in *The Bankers' Almanack*) showing the last returns of banks and their existing note-issue. Thus collectors can divide them into large circulation banks and small circulation banks (although many banks which had succumbed before the Act are not always traceable).

They are valued as follows (for VF condition):

Large circulation banks:	£12 – £20
Small circulation banks:	£15 – £40
Unsigned (unissued) notes:	£10 – £30

In very worn state these notes are obtainable at much less.

Something like a hundred of these provincial banks still have their notes honoured because they amalgamated into banking firms which still function today.

Barclays, for example, was originally formed by twenty such banks and added many more as the firm grew. (The founding firm,

In 1825 and 1826 Bank of England £1 notes of 1821 were overprinted for re-issue. They were the last issues of £1 notes by the Bank of England until 1928

Barclay, Bevan, Tritton, Ransom, Bouverie and Co., traces its own history to the goldsmith John Freame of Lombard Street).

These notes are often found in worn condition, but in Fine condition they fetch £30 over face, and in Crisp condition they fetch £50 over face.

Unlike stamps and coins, early banknotes in worn condition are acceptable to collectors. No one, at the time of issue, bought them to put aside and keep as specimens.

Bank of England notes were issued as follows:

1695   £10, £20, £30, £40, £50, £100.   No prices recorded.

Later the amount was filled in by hand, the first issue being withdrawn because of forgery.

1697   Watermarked paper.   Value not recorded.

All notes until 1700 had the payee's name inserted by hand. Then staff names were used. Notes signed by Edward Clarke and John Miller are known among the earlier issues.

Notes of later periods are more easily available to collectors. They all have the rough appearance of the familiar White Fiver which went out of circulation only in 1956.

1798-1825.   For VF condition:

£1 Abraham Newland   £150   £1 Henry Hase   £150

Notes issued after 1826 no longer have the signatures hand-written.

Branch notes are known (in the order in which the branches were founded) from:

Gloucester, Manchester, Birmingham, Bristol, Liverpool, Leeds, Exeter, Swansea, Plymouth, Cardiff, Belfast, Leicester, Hull, Norwich, Newcastle, Portsmouth, Southampton.

Notes issued from branches are at least twice as rare as those of the London Bank. Branches ceased note issues of their own in 1939. Apart from a £1000 note of Hull, branches only made issues of denominations up to £100.

Naturally all Bank of England notes, although not necessarily legal tender any longer, are valid, and will be cashed by the Bank of England. All notes up to the twentieth century are rare.

From 1900 values are as follows, for VF condition:

£1 notes	Signed by		
1928	C. P. Mahon	Green	£9
1929–34	B. G. Catterns	Green	£8
1934–49	K. P. Peppiatt	Green	£6
		Light blue	£5
		Dark blue	£7
		Green post war	£8
		Green with metal strip	£5
1949–55	P. S. Beale	Green (strip)	£4
1955–62	L. K. O'Brien	Green (strip)	£4
1960	L. K. O'Brien	Queen's head	£2.10.
1962–6	J. Q. Hollom	,, small notes	£3
1966–	J. S. Fforde	,,	£1

10s. notes were normally printed at a ratio of 1 to 7 £1 notes.
They are generally estimated at up to 50 per cent more than £1 notes of the same signature.

World War I made large issues of paper money essential. At the beginning paper was in short supply and the Treasury were obliged to use paper normally reserved for printing stamps. Thus the first Treasury notes have the watermarks of well-known postage stamps of the period. They are known as 'Bradburys' after Sir John Bradbury (later Lord Bradbury) the Permanent Secretary to the Treasury, who signed them. For VF condition:

First issue £1	(August 1914)	with stamp paper watermark. Black and white	£40
10s.		Red and white	£45
Second issue £1		Black and white	£25
10s.		Red and white	£30
£1	(October 1914)	Black and white	£25
		Gallipoli overprint	£90
10s.	(Jan. 1915)	Red and white	£50
		Gallipoli overprint	£70
Third issue £1	(Feb. 1917)	Green and brown.	£8
10s.	(Nov. 1918)	Serial No. Red.	£9
		Serial No. Black.	£11

Treasury notes signed by Warren Fisher.

First issue £1	(Oct. 1919)	Overall watermark.	£6
10s.			£12
Second issue £1	1923	Square watermark.	£5
10s.		'No.' deleted from serial number.	£8
Third issue £1	1928	Titled 'Great Britain and Northern Ireland'.	£8
10s.		,, ,,	£10

5s. notes of 1919 were not officially circulated but some got into circulation.	£300
2s. 6d. notes are not known. Dieproofs. George V vignette	£50

Today only the Bank of England can issue banknotes in England. But this regulation does not apply to Scotland, where notes of £1 and over may be issued by certain banks. The first banknotes of Scotland were issued by the Bank of Scotland, shortly after the Bank of England's first issues. They were followed by the Royal Bank of Scotland in 1727, the British Linen Bank in 1746, and then a succession of banks.

In 1777 a one guinea note was issued which may well be the first colour note in Great Britain. Produced by the Royal Bank of Scotland, it is on a blue background and has George III's head in red. The Bank's record books show it as the 'Red Head Issue'.

All early £1 notes of Scotland are valued at £30-£50, except for the Red Head Issue at £70. For higher denominations, add face value.

A great variety of more modern Scottish notes exist. Those of the early part of the twentieth century are 'square' shaped and usually very colourful.

£1 notes in circulated condition are valued at £8, in crisp condition £12.

Private banknotes first appeared in Ireland in 1783 and by 1927 a number of important banks were making note issues, namely the Bank of Ireland, National Bank Ltd, Munster and Leinster Bank, Hibernian Bank, Ulster Bank Ltd, Royal Bank of Ireland, Provincial Bank of Ireland, and Northern Bank Ltd.

They are valued approximately the same as Scottish notes.

Isle of Man notes are particularly interesting in that private banknotes were being issued up until 1961, as the Bank Charter Act did not affect them. Too few have come on the market to establish values.

The Channel Islands also have an interesting history for paper money collectors and the most sought-after sets of notes are those of the German occupation. Guernsey produced £1 and 10s. dated 1943 without the German authority in readiness for British re-occupation. These liberation notes are among the rarest of the C. I. modern issues.

It is said that a German sentry was actually stationed in the printing room in Guernsey and did not realise what was being printed.

The Guernsey issue of 1943:		2s. 6d.	£8
£1 black	£35	1s. 3d.	£4
10s.	£45	1s.	£4
5s.	£12	6d.	£4

It must be understood that this is only a rough guide to prices. There are many exceptions and in some cases notes have sold at widely differing prices making it difficult to estimate the proper value. Notes in EF condition fetch very much more than the prices for VF.

It must also be remembered that there are many varieties. Even the first issue Bradbury notes are found in three major varieties owing to differences in type etc. of the serial numbers. One such variety is worth at least twice as much as the commoner issue.

The best guide to values is the Stanley Gibbons catalogue – the first full catalogue of British paper money to be published.

4 world war II

Among modern notes the most interesting are usually found to be the issues of war-time. This is because often there is not time to mint coins, or a shortage of the necessary metals. The result is a mass of emergency paper money which more often than not has no counterpart in coinage and therefore tells the story of war better than any other collecting media.

It is probably true to say that more specialists go in for the notes of World War II than for those of any other war or subject. Several catalogues have been produced specifically related to note issues of the war. The most notable are *World War II Axis Military Currency* by Raymond S. Toy and Bob Meyer, and *World War II Allied Military Currency* by Raymond S. Toy.

Normally this type of paper money can be put into three categories. First, issues made by occupied countries under the direction of the conquerors, which replaced the normal day-to-day currency and now tell the story of inflation or military occupation. Secondly, the purely military notes issued for soldiers or for invasion and occupation, bearing testimony to the event. Finally there are the notes of concentration camps, prisoner-of-war camps, partisan issues, etc., which are vividly connected with the effect of war.

So vast is the overall field that many collectors specialise in one category or even in the issues of one country. The notes issued by the Japanese for occupation of former British and Dutch colonies and for parts of China run into many hundreds.

Some of the notes issued during the war are of definitive importance to historians. These are the issues which were used for propaganda purposes or to incite the enemy to change sides. It was the practice of both Axis and Allied forces to print paper money on one side of the paper and a propaganda message, on the other. This usually took the form of forging the enemy's paper money and telling the recipients that it would become worthless in a short time. Another use was to turn one side of a banknote into a safe-conduct pass. This practice is still carried on in Vietnam, and was very successfully carried out by the United Nations forces in Korea. When Germany invaded Czechoslovakia in 1939 a large quantity of paper money had already been printed for normal circulation by the Czechs. The Germans now used this money and it can be found overprinted by hand and by machine.

Collectors will soon come across Bohemia-Moravia notes (German-occupied Czechoslovakia) perforated 'Specimen'. These were produced specially for collectors by the Czechs after the war.

The thoroughness associated with German control was evident in their own war-time currency notes. By order of the Supreme Army Commander (23 September 1939) special notes known as *Reichskreditkassen* were printed for circulation in all occupied territories.

The Wehrmacht had its own paper money too. There were two basic types. *Behelfszahlungsmittel* – auxiliary payment certificates which were undated and printed on one side only – and *Verrechnungsscheine* – reckoning notes.

Auxiliary payment certificates were issued to German soldiers and were valued at ten times face. But not when a civilian re-presented it! The 1 Reichspfennig with a monogram watermark instead of stars is very rare. The British were not slow in making propaganda out of these notes to the luckless civilian population who were losing ten to one on the notes. They were forged in Britain and the plain reverse had poetry added – some of it obscene. The usual message was '50 pfennig heiss' ich – Um 4·50 bescheiss' ich, Jedermann, der denkt, Dass Hitler ihm was schenkt'. It means '50 pfennig is my name – I'll cheat everyone of 4·50 who thinks Hitler gives him something'. These were dropped by planes over Germany.

Ich bin Hitlers Arschwisch.
Keiner nimmt mich an,
Weil sich niemand etwas
Für mich kaufen kann.

50 Pfennig heiss' ich –
Um 4.50 bescheiss' ich
Jedermann, der denkt,
Dass Hitler ihm was schenkt.

Verrechnungsschein notes were given to German troops as they embarked for occupied territories. They were then exchanged for circulating money in the occupied territory when the soldiers arrived.

In the case of the occupation of Greece, auxiliary payment certificates were hand-stamped on the reverse with circular marks, one showing the German Eagle and the other the Greek coat of arms.

When Italy marched to war Mussolini planned to divide Egypt into two nations. Egypt would have Cairo as its capital and an enlarged Sudan would have Khartoum as capital. Notes were printed for the intended occupation and are extremely rare. Those for Egypt, 'Cassa Mediterranea per L'Egitto', never got further than the printing works as Italian forces reeled before their adversaries. Only a few are known to be in collectors' hands, and almost as rare are the notes 'Cassa Mediterranea per il Sudan'.

In Poland a rare note is the 100 zloty Bank of Poland which was overprinted in red 'Generalgouvernement für die besetzten polnischen Gebiete'. Such notes only circulated for a few months.

Croatia under the Germans issued a new monetary unit, the Kuna, and denominations from 1 to 1000 were printed in the Giesecke Printing Works, Berlin. Collectors particularly seek the 20 and 50 Kuna notes dated January 1944, as these were never put into circulation because of partisan action. The train carrying the notes was destroyed by the partisans and the whole lot destroyed except for a few kept by the partisans as souvenirs.

In Montenegro the government officials fled to the mountains with a convoy of paper money. They hid the money in caves and continued their flight on foot. Wide-awake peasants living in the neighbourhood soon located them and when the Italians marched

Opposite Verrechnungsschein notes. They were changed for circulating money by German soldiers when they arrived in the occupied territories

in to occupy the territory they were surprised at the enormous wealth of the peasant population – until they found out what had happened. All notes were called in and examined. Those that did not come from the hidden money (the Italians got the serial numbers from the national bank) were overprinted with a circular handstamp 'Verificato' (Verified) and permitted to continue in circulation.

The Germans had continual trouble from the Yugoslavs and the Montenegrins and at one stage used old 100 dinar notes of Yugoslavia changed to read '100 people' and stating that safe conduct would be guaranteed for every 100 men who surrendered with their arms to the German Army.

The enormous range of notes issued under Japanese direction is dealt with in the chapter on Japanese notes, but some deserve special mention. One of the early Federal Reserve Bank of China notes, designed by a Chinese engraver under Japanese orders, was to have a vignette of a famous Chinese sage. The engraver designed his hand to make a reversed 'V' sign, intending it as an insult to the Japanese. This was quickly altered once the Japanese realised what was happening – along with a number of other notes into which engravers worked various anti-Japanese signs.

Among the occupation notes the Japanese produced for the Pacific and Burma areas are some Allied propaganda notes. Philippine notes were overprinted 'The Co-Prosperity Sphere: What is it Worth?'. Forgeries also exist and some notes are found with both Japanese and English text reading: 'Passed by Censor, Japanese Military Police'. These are flagrant forgeries and nothing like them was ever used by the Japanese. Indeed one of the first things they did was to remove all signs of the English language from banknotes.

Federal Reserve Bank of China note with reversed V sign

The British used the Malaya 10 dollar occupation note for propaganda, using three languages on the reverse: Malay, Burmese and Chinese. The text reads: 'At present in Malaya, Japanese money is not recognised and the original notes are the only valid legal tender. When the British return to Malaya, their notes will be used as before. Japanese notes will disappear together with the Japanese, forever, and the original British money will be used forever'.

Allied military paper money included a whole range of notes which, because of the enormous quantities needed, were printed by various firms and in various countries. The bulk came from the United States but the Bureau of Engraving and Printing, unable to cope with all the work, contracted Forbes Lithograph Co. of Boston and Stecher-Traung Lithograph Co. of San Francisco whose notes can often be detected by the inclusion of the letters 'F' or 'S' in the scrollwork.

Military currency for Austria was printed in England and the United States. It can be identified by the watermarks. The British has a wavy line watermark and the American the words 'Military Authority' repeated.

Allied military currency for France caused an uproar because of the words *'Emis en France'*. General de Gaulle took exception to the statement 'issued in France' and the use of the tricolour on the reverse. The next issue of notes had the word 'France' on the reverse instead of the flag to appease him. The top denomination,

Japanese occupation money had for the first serial letter the letter standing for the country of occupation. This note 'MO' is for Malaya, others were issued for 'P' Philippines, 'B' Burma, 'O' Oceania etc. There were so many of them that combat troops referred to them as 'Mickey Mouse' and 'Banana' money

5000 francs, of the first issue was never issued because forgeries were found a short time before the note was due to go into circulation.

Each packet of notes had a wrapper on which, in English and French, an explanation was given of replacement notes: 'If the numbers on the notes in this package do not run in sequence, the substituted notes are identified by an 'x' printed thereon'. The 'x' appears near the serial number.

Identification of the zone of issue of military notes for Germany is made by examining the serial number. The first digit in the serial number is the key. If it is '1' then the note is for the United States Zone. 'O' indicates the British Zone and 'OO' the French Zone. There is a difficulty in identifying Russian Zone notes which have a dash before the number. It so happens that the United States also used a dash to indicate a replacement note. The plates were sent to Russia from the United States Bureau, so where collectors have notes with the letter 'F' for Forbes Lithograph Co. and the dash it is clearly an American replacement note. The Russians later replaced the dash with a '1'.

Allied military currency issued in Italy was in lire denominations from 5 to 1000. Sometimes collectors find quite clever forgeries, as many people would alter the value of a note by adding a hand-drawn 'O' after the denomination – turning a 100 lire note into a 1,000 lire note!

Notes for Japan were kept in circulation for longer than any

British Army issues used in Africa

other occupied territory, in fact starting in 1945 and lasting until 1958. This gave rise to many types and varieties and in 1950 the notes were printed by Japan.

Belgium had a special liberation issue printed by Bradbury Wilkinson in 1943 and also produced notes for army use only in 1946 headed 'Armée Belge'. It was a serious offence for a civilian to be found in possession of these notes.

British Army notes for use in North Africa and Greece and Tripolitania are getting scarcer. The North Africa notes are in sterling and the £1 is the rarest of the series. Both types of note have a lion on crown vignette.

The normal issues of India bearing the head of George VI can be found with overprints in both black and red: 'Military Administration of Burma – Legal tender in Burma only'.

Hong Kong, which saw some emergency notes at the beginning of the Japanese occupation, saw a special issue in September 1945 of which the top denominations, 1, 5 and 10 dollars, are all rare. The one dollar yellow on white was printed by machines using power provided by the British submarine.

An unusual situation developed in Réunion where both Vichy and the Free French used the same emergency paper money – small notes marked 'Banque de la Réunion' and signed by the same person. In the case of the Free French notes, however, the cross of Lorraine was added.

Liberated countries did not always appreciate the 'liberation' issues and the Netherlands did not approve of the notes issued to

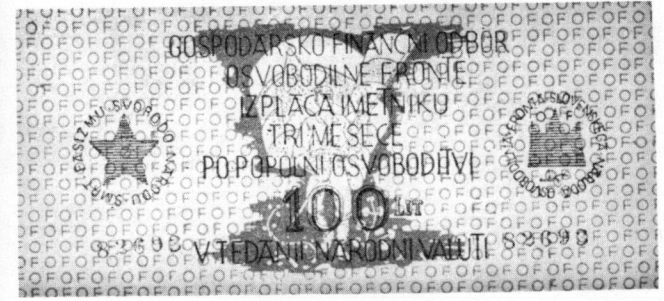

Partisan Slovak issue with 'Death to Fascism' motto

American troops. They were withdrawn after just over three months circulation.

The gallant force of Norwegians under Major-General Steffens issued special Norwegian State promissory notes while they were encircled by German troops at Voss. Steffens had sought permission to do this from the Norges Bank and all these notes are extremely rare.

There are many other interesting notes of the period and some of the prisoner of war notes, hand-made by prisoners as well as officially produced ones, are highly prized by collectors. In addition there is a vast range of post-war military payment certificates. All United States military bases in Britain use such notes and they are frequently changed to avoid forgery.

A considerable number of different partisan notes were issued which are also in demand among collectors.

In northern Greece partisans issued national bonds which were used to pay civilians for 'appropriated' provisions. These notes were by authority of the 'Civil Committee for National Liberation'.

In Montenegro the wily partisans issued special notes with diminishing value. Each month the notes would be worth a little less. This was to ensure that they circulated.

Slovak partisans printed their own paper money in the woods and emblazoned on them 'Death to Fascism'.

Few areas of the hobby encompass such a vivid association with the great events of World War II, and it is one of the most popular specialist fields.

5 european paper money

france

Of all the world's old paper money the *assignats* of the French Revolution are still the most common. There are some extremely rare notes of this period but the commoner types are available to collectors for about a pound, which considering their great age and historic significance is inexpensive by any standard.

The man who thought up the idea of *assignats* never lived to see them used. He was John Law, a Scotsman who developed a mathematical genius. Incredibly, he put his talents to work in the gambling dens and soon had a reputation as a lady-killer. An affair with one woman led to a duel in which John Law killed his adversary. Subsequently he was sentenced to death for murder, but managed to buy his escape and turned up in France, quickly to make his mark in the gambling dens. It was in a gambling saloon that he met the Duke of Orleans who was so impressed that he later entrusted the financial affairs of his nation to Law.

Law stated: 'What I propose is to make a land currency equal to the value of the land and to the value of actual coined money without being subject, as is coined money, to a fall in value.' Saint-Simon, of the Council of Finance and a member of the Council of the Regency, blocked Law's proposals, and the best Law could obtain was a charter for a private bank which he opened on 2 May 1716, the Banque Générale. Because his note-issue could not be modified by royal edict it became very popular and later the Banque Générale was converted into a state bank.

A contemporary illustrated list of *assignats* exists showing coloured pictures of many rare notes. The inscription by the printer reads: 'Septembre 1796/(Ou le 15 Fructidor an 4 ième de la R.e F.e/ A Paris/Chez Bance, Graveur, rue St Sévérin, No. 115'.

As well as the State notes Bance described some of the Billets de Confiance which were issued until 1792 by a large number of cities, 'Caisses Patriotiques' and others, including private citizens notes used throughout the whole of France.

Only the notes of Paris are shown by Bance. We find Caisse Patriotique (signed by Buquet and Vitallis) 18.5.1791 5 livres in white; 15.5.1791 25 livres in yellow; May 1791 in blue, and others in pink and even violet. We also find Compagnie de Commission, rue des Bons Enfans 5, 8, 10, 20 sols, brown. These notes were printed on parchment in brown colour. Even rarer are the Maison de Secours, Rue des Filles St. Thomas 1.9.1791, 20 sols in red, 30 sols yellow, 40 sols white and 10 sols blue.

As well as these special notes of Paris, Bance also, strangely perhaps, shows the notes from the siege of Mayence, where the French occupation forces, besieged by a German army, issued notes in different denominations and dates.

This fascinating print by Bance is of great interest to collectors for various reasons. Not only does it show us many notes which were not known to exist before, but it gives us a short history of the monetary evolution in France during the Revolution, and it demonstrates that already at that time there were paper money collectors in France.

The first issue of *assignats* was for 4,000 million francs, each note being for 100 francs and bearing interest at the rate of 5 per cent. In 1790 interest was reduced to 3 per cent and a second issue of 800 million francs was issued carrying no interest and declared by law to be legal tender.

Had the *assignat* system stopped there, as was strongly advocated by Mirabeau, there is no reason why the notes should not have been successful, but further issues brought the total up to 3,750 million. Depreciation followed and a 100 franc note became worth 20 francs in coin. Protective legislation was passed giving as much as twenty-years' imprisonment for traders who differentiated between goods sold for coin as against *assignats*. These severe measures were only relaxed after the fall of Robespierre.

By June 1794 a total of 8,000 million francs had been issued of which only 2,464 million had been redeemed by the Treasury. By 1796 issues brought the total to 45,500 million and they became virtually worthless.

It was the practice of the revolutionaries to have many different people sign the *assignats*. The most humble and common *assignat*, the 5 livres dated 10 Brumaire An 2 (31 October 1793) can be found with a hundred different signatures. A complete collection is extremely rare, as also are uncut sheets – the notes were printed in sheets of ten. As with the collecting of imperforate stamps, collectors seek wide margins and these are difficult to obtain in the Brumaire notes. Mostly they are found with borders cut close to the design, yet the original borders were over an inch wide.

The hundred signatories of the Brumaire notes are: Arriquez, Arnoux, Audin, Augee, Auguste, Aze, Baillet, Bancey, Barba, Baron, Bazière, Berlioz, Bertaut, Bertier, Bertin, Beurlier, Blanche, Bot, Brout, Brouz, Bruron, Busier, Chaigner, Coipel, Convième, David, Davion Denis, Deperthe, Didier, D'Osseville, Drouet, Duboc, Dubois, Declos, Du Flog, Dumez, Dutour, Duval (two different signatures), Duverger, Emon, Faure, Fenix, Feuillade, Fontaine, Gouquet, Galland, Gaudet, Gerard, Gillet, Gilliero, Gomez, Gourgaud, Goust, Guinand, Henriot, Jeanneau, Labrosse, La Chapelle, Lacroix, Lambert (two different signatures), Laporte, Lasceux, Le Court, Lenoir, Loegel, Loiseau, Loiseleau, Loquet, Luillier, Martin, Mauge, Mauroy, Megnie, Mercier, Michau, Mixelle, Momoro, Mortier, Palale, Petitain, Picot, Poidevin, Police, Poullain, Preux, Regnier, Riotto, Rolin, Roussel, Sal, Sanche, Schrantz, Semen, Symon, Throuin, Troupe, Vauchy.

Early *assignats* are known as 'royal *assignats*' because they showed the king's head, but this was soon dispensed with, as was the head of the king. Collectors sometimes find rare 'Royal' watermarks in *assignats*, usually used in error.

At a time when the louis d'or sold on the black market for 15,000 francs and paper money had depreciated 97 per cent, the Minister of Finance, Ramel Nogaret, proposed the creation of a new banknote to replace the *assignats* and thus rescue France.

This was the territorial mandat. On 18 March 1796, 2,400 million promissory notes were issued and the Government proposed to exchange 30 francs *assignats* against one franc territorial mandat.

Their depreciation was even more rapid than that of the *assignats* and on 4 February 1797 the printing plates were broken up in public in a symbolic ceremony.

France went on in its later history to develop a distinctive paper money in that it is colourful and bright. The vivid colours of French paper money are even more prominent in the paper money of its colonies and are widely collected.

germany

Early notes of the many states which came to form Germany as we know it today are all rare. Gradually the Reichsbank took over the note-issuing rights of the German states and by 1914 only four other banks were issuing notes: Badische Bank, Bayerische Notenbank, Sachsische Bank and Württembergische Notenbank. These banks continued to issue notes until 1935.

When World War I broke out a shortage of cash necessitated the use of emergency paper money for small denominations, known to collectors as *Notgeld*.

The early issues are plain and often hand-signed by local magistrates. Denominations of 50 pfg. and 1, 2 and 5 marks were those mostly in use. This first issue was retired when the *Darlehnskassen* (loan notes) were produced by the authorities and it was no longer necessary for towns to issue their own notes.

For a while only state money circulated, except in Alsace which was under partial French occupation. A few communities issued notes throughout the war to pay for state relief. As they had no revenue these notes were only redeemed after the war and are all exceedingly rare.

By 1916 another shortage of small change had occurred because of the rising price of silver – which exceeded the nominal value of the coin. Everyone began hoarding silver. The city of Strasbourg later admitted that it had stored away six million marks in silver in the council safes. *Notgeld* was issued to make up for the deficiency in values of 5, 10, 25 and 50 pfg. The emergency was, however, not as great as that of 1914 and the authorities of local councils and large factories had more time to prepare designs.

It was soon found that people were collecting the pretty pictures, for by now just about every town and city, even police stations and factories, were issuing notes. The revenue to be derived from collectors was quickly appreciated and some German cities introduced odd denominations like 60, 75, 80 and 90 pfg., just for collectors. Then some cities began issuing whole sets of notes with perhaps twelve different 50 pfg. notes all illustrating a local legend or even a fairy tale.

At that time some 10,000 collectors of these notes bombarded council officials for examples of the various notes and when it became apparent that many councils were issuing notes merely to sell them to collectors the Reichstag stepped in on 17 September 1922 with a general prohibition order. Even so, notes still appeared for some time in contravention of the order.

Some famous signatures can be found on *Notgeld*. Dr Adenauer's signature appears on the notes of Cologne. Collectors find it hard to obtain examples of the 1914 emergency money and some of the earlier issues of the second emergency money issue which were genuinely used as money are hard to find. But the second issue lasted from 1916 to September 1922 and only the earlier notes were genuinely used for emergency. However, the glut of later notes has in the course of time become absorbed by the growing band of collectors. Today *Notgeld* is not so common as it once was and is likely to become much scarcer. It is possible to make theme collections, illustrating German history and politics, through these colourful small notes.

The following numbers are believed to exist:

1914 issue:	452 cities issued	5,600 different notes
1916-22	3,900 cities issued	26,120
1921-22	serial notes	12,000

At the end of the war prices started rising rapidly and the Reichsbank saw the necessity to issue a new type of *Notgeld* but this time in mark denominations instead of the small-change pfennigs. Unfortunately for them, a strike interrupted their plans and they hastily invited the larger towns and cities to print their own notes again in values of 5, 10, 20 and 50 marks.

Known as *Grossgeldscheine* (they were reckoned in gold), these notes were plain and the Reichsbank went so far as to agree to pay half of any loss incurred by a town through forgery – and in fact in some instances did so. When the Reichsbank was able to release its own 50 mark notes the *Grossgeldscheine* were retired. Many of these are still found with official cancellations. This is because collectors asked local authorities if they could buy the notes at less than face value after their official retirement.

But the economic situation did not improve. Within a short time the Reichsbank had to issue higher value notes including eight different 1,000 mark notes. They again had to ask towns and cities to issue notes, and in 1922 the 'cheque notes' appeared, so called because the text states that a bank would pay the face value of the note as soon as normal circulation was restored.

It looked as if the situation might be saved – then the French army marched into the Rhine and Ruhr industrial areas. The value of the mark took a drop and continued to drop. On one occasion the value of a note dropped by half in a single day. The Reichsbank printers were unable to cope with the volume of printing needed to keep up a supply of notes. So the government printers supplied plates and watermarked paper to some ninety private printers who were asked to help out. It is believed that over 400,000 plates were used. The Reichsbank also overprinted notes with new and higher denominations, and one issue, that for Kreis Rastenburg, was overprinted twice on the same note.

The highest denomination was the 100 billion note which, during its life, was worth just over £7.

At its peak the inflation saw wages being paid daily and staff allowed time off during the day in order to buy their shopping before inflation destroyed their wages.

The Great Notes (*Grossgeldscheine*) of 1918-19 were issued by 624 cities etc. with over 4,260 types. There were 3,600 types of inflation notes issued in 1922 and this figure rose to an astounding 59,800 in 1923.

Germany's monetary problems recovered in 1924 with the use of Karl Helfferich's proposals for the new unit, the Rentenmark – based on the old Danish monetary reform which had worked during the Napoleonic inflation.

Collectors of war-notes are often surprised to find that Germany issued some 5,000 different prisoner-of-war notes during World War I. With the advent of World War II special war-notes were issued to German troops for exchanging into currency in occupied territories. These had to be changed at special rates which were hardly advantageous to the occupied territory. The British Government was not slow to forge these notes (which had plain reverses) and to imprint upon the reverse a rude rhyme about Adolf Hitler and what his paper money was fit for. These were dropped by aeroplane.

Collectors who like quantity will find Germany one of the better attractions. Since 1914 the nation has issued well over 125,000 different notes illustrating the greatest upheavals of the twentieth century.

hungary

Louis Kossuth is to this day acclaimed as the greatest Hungarian patriot and his paper money issues unfold the story of the vain freedom war of Hungary. When the independence war broke out against the Emperor of Austria, hereditary King of Hungary, in 1848, the 'Kamatos utalvany' interest-paying legal tender treasury bills were issued. They were signed by Volgyi Ferenc and Endrey under the authorisation of Louis Kossuth as Finance Minister. The 50 forint can be found light blue or yellow; the 100 forint

This page and facing page Kossuth Independence issues with which he hoped to raise money

light brown or pink, and the 500 forint light grey in two sizes. Only three 500 forint notes are known.

These notes were intended to raise capital for the Hungarian National Bank – the National Bank of Austria no longer supporting the regime.

The second issue of notes was by the Hungarian Commercial Bank, (Magyar Kereskedelmi Bank) and the notes bear the signature of 'Kossuth Lajos', Minister of Finance. They comprised fractional notes of one sixteenth, one eighth, quarter and half and 1 forint and 2 forint notes.

By now metal coin was in very short supply and a third issue was made dated 1 September 1848. These were 'Penzjegy' (state notes). There were two distinct 5 forint notes, a 10 forint and a 100 forint note. This issue had to be followed by a new issue of fractional notes owing to the almost total disappearance of small change. The new notes dated 1 January 1849 are known as 'Kinctari utalvany' and consisted of 15 and 30 pengos, signed by Volgyi Ferenc under the National Honved – defence committee.

As the Allied armies of Austria and Russia drove deeper into Hungarian territory the constitutional government escaped to Debrecen and there issued new 'Kincstari utalvany' 2 pengo forint notes dated 1 July 1849, signed by Louis Kossuth as Governor of Hungary and Ferenc Duschek as Minister of Finance. These notes went into circulation on 26 July.

The last issue of Kossuth notes made in Hungary was issued from Szeged and Arad (south Hungary) dated 'Budapesten 1849-ki julius l-en'. They went into circulation during the last month of the Freedom War of Hungary, August, and consisted of 2 and 10 pengo notes. Both are extremely rare. Austrian forces refused to redeem Kossuth notes and they were collected up and burned (sixty million florins' worth of notes were burned).

But Louis Kossuth had by no means given up his cause. Seeking refuge in the United States he issued promissory notes for the Independent Hungarian Government – with the permission of the United States authorities. These were for 1, 5, 10, 50 and 100 dollars. The two high denominations were hand-signed by Kossuth. Issued in 1852 they were followed by another issue of U.S. notes from Philadelphia but in the Hungarian language, and for denominations 1, 2 and 5 forints.

In 1860 Kossuth came to London, still determined in his cause, and issued notes in the Hungarian language for 1, 2 and 5 forints. But the Austrian Emperor made a direct complaint to the British Government and the issue was confiscated and burned – naturally, a few specimens escaped destruction and found their way to collectors.

Louis Kossuth, the champion of liberty, never gave up hope, and as late as 1866, when the political situation looked hopeful, new plates were made for Hungarian notes by his sons. Original printings of these notes are unknown but reprints exist of 2, 10 garas and 1 magyar.

In 1948, the centenary of the war, the Hungarian National Museum staged a special exhibition of related material and reprinted from the original plate the 2 pengo forint 'Kincstari utalvany' dated 1 July 1849 (which had been printed in Debrecen and Szeged). The reverse, however, had an inscription added: 'Keszitette a Magyar Nemzeti Museum 1948 etc.'

The Kossuth issue in England had an interesting side-effect on history. The reception of Kossuth by Lord Palmerston and the encouragement given to him was a subject of one of the charges of independent action made against Palmerston which caused his political downfall.

Hungary suffered one of the worst inflations the world has ever

This war-time issue of Hungary, dated 1943, shows the engraver's skill at its best

seen shortly after the end of World War II. The war had, of course, caused the country to suffer inflation but in 1945 came what collectors term the second Hungarian inflation, 1945-6. The first post-war notes were released on 16 July 1945 but rapidly lost value as a result of inflation so that more and more were necessary. By 18 March 1946 notes were printed for 100,000,000 pengoe. At this stage the monetary unit was changed to milpengoe and this too suffered a similar fate so that on 3 June 1946 it was changed to yet another unit, the bilpengoe. One bilpengoe now equalled 1,000 million old pengoe. But inflation continued its course and notes appeared for 100 million bilpengoe. The dates on the notes no longer had any meaning as these were dated 3 June 1946.

The government decided that the only thing left to do was to change the monetary unit again. This time it was the adopengoe or tax-pengoe. The ratio at one time was nothing less than two million bilpengoe for one adopengoe. The highest adopengoe note issued was for 100 million and therefore equalled 20,000,000,000,000,000,000,000,000,000 pengoe!

At the same time tax-stamps overprinted were used as currency.

italy

Large colourful notes of Italy are well known in Britain where many soldiers brought home wads of high denomination lire as souvenirs. Indeed one British patrol accepted the surrender of an entire convoy carrying military pay for an Italian army.

But collectors find it much harder to trace the early issues of Italy. Italy was not unified until 1870 and prior to that date independent kingdoms or states issued paper money. The principal area issuing notes was the Papal States ruled over by the Pope as absolute monarch as well as titular head of the Catholic Church. As the unification programme moved ahead under Garibaldi, Cavour and others, the Pope lost control of these lands and it was not until 1929 when Benito Mussolini granted land to the Pope that the Vatican City was created.

Notes were also issued from the Kingdom of Piedmont which was ruled over by the House of Savoy; Victor Emmanuel II was also King of Sardinia so the two territories were joined.

The largest area of Italy was the Kingdom of the Two Sicilies created in 1759 when Naples and Sicily were united.

Lombardy-Venetia, another considerable area, was controlled by Austrian forces from 1815 to 1866. At one time Venice broke free from Austrian control, declared itself independent, and issued special banknotes, 'Moneta Patrioica'.

Parma, Modena, Lucca, San Marino and Tuscany may also have issued notes at various times, but evidence is not always available.

During the war of 1939–45 Italy issued notes for the conquest of Egypt and the Sudan in readiness for the occasion (as described on page 46). But, owing to the inability of the Italians to defeat the Allied armies, these notes are extremely rare.

poland

Very attractive and large notes of Poland issued at the time of World War II are among the most inexpensive notes available to collectors, for this nation was severely ravaged by the occupying Axis powers and its economy deliberately ruined.

It is perhaps strange that Poland's first issue of notes was made under similar circumstances and remains testimony to Poland's forlorn struggle for independence. The first partition of Poland was caused by King Frederick of Prussia who arranged with his neighbours in 1772 to have parts of Poland. Russia took the largest area, Austria a sizeable share and Prussia the most valuable part. The Polish Diet continued to meet even though they had lost a third of their population overnight, and effected reforms. The Diet converted the elected monarchy into an hereditary monarchy with the Elector of Saxony as successor to the throne. Prussia and Austria accepted this – but not Russia. This led to war in 1794 and now the Poles found a real leader in Thaddeus Kosciuszko – who had fought with George Washington in the War of Independence against Britain. Considering the numerical superiority and enormous trained armies pitted against Poland it was surprising that Poland did so well – winning quite a few important battles with little more than peasants and noblemen joined in a common cause.

Prussian and Russian armies settled the fate of Poland at the battles of Szczekociny, Praga and Maciejowice. The war started in March 1794 and as Kosciuszko had no finances he issued special paper money to back the insurrection. The rebellion was firmly crushed in November 1794 and these notes are all that remain. They turn up in extremely fine condition more than they do in worn condition. Even so they are rare. The text states: '…which the National Treasury will pay out of the funds for the backing of the designated Treasury Notes and for the universal mortgaged National Welfare to each bearer of the actual note, and will be accepted as well for all public revenues according to the foregoing resolution of the Highest Council of the Nation'. The term 'Grzywna Kolonska' on the notes refers to a kind of international weight for assaying gold in use at the time. Notes for 5, 10, 25, 50 and 100 zloty were issued.

portugal

An interesting country for collectors. Its present currency is printed by Bradbury, Wilkinson and Co. who are probably the largest security printers in the world. Today's Portuguese paper money is colourful and stable, but that nation's paper money affairs were not always so safe.

Indeed the greatest 'forgery' of paper money the world has ever seen, other than the Nazi forgeries, took place in the 1920's when some well-organised criminals decided not to counterfeit the

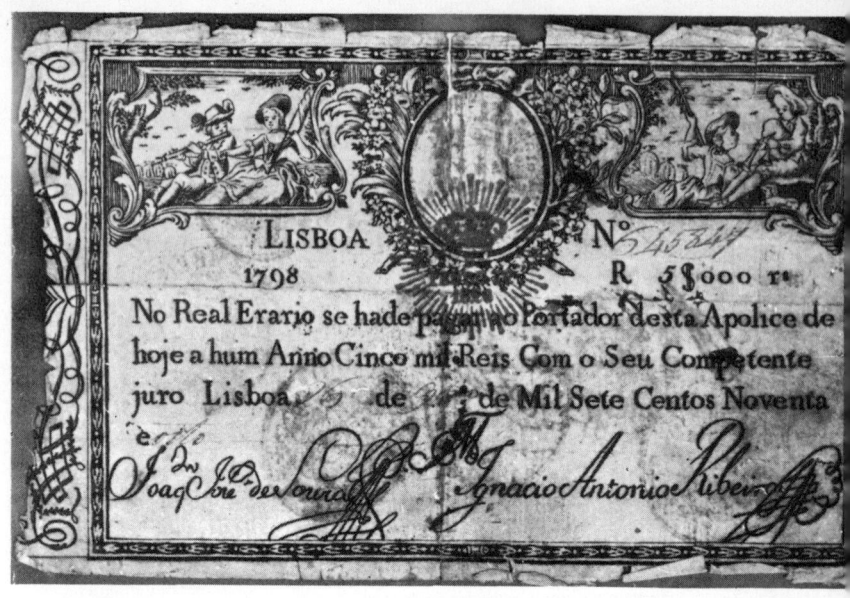

War of the Two Brothers note overprinted for the expected return of Pedro IV from Brazil 1826

banknotes but to simply counterfeit the orders to the printing house of Waterlow and Sons. The printers were given the impression that a huge quantity of notes was required to be printed off existing plates and that they would be overprinted 'Angola' in Portugal – but that it all had to be kept quiet for political reasons at that stage. At all events the bait was taken and the notes reprinted. The forgers even had the audacity to go back for more – and got them. Naturally the Bank of Portugal became aware that there were many more notes in circulation than there should have been. Study them how they would, however, they were all perfect – until one clerk spotted a serial number error and checks were made with the printers. The balloon went up. It is noteworthy that the chief instigator of the plot had at that time reached such prominence in the Bank of Portugal that he was due to be made president and confidently anticipated being in a position to be able to destroy any incriminating evidence within four months; as it was, he was arrested and imprisoned. The case brought international repercussions and nearly bankrupted the printers who had to pay Portugal an indemnity.

Portugal's early paper money is equally interesting and presents the collector with one of the many examples where condition cannot be 'mint' because paper money of the War of the Two Brothers (Pedro IV and Miguel I) was used for over thirty years, overprinted and officially repaired by banks. Paper money collectors, unlike stamp collectors, cannot always expect to be able to get items in new condition.

Notes dated 1798–1805 were overprinted by the two brothers as late as 1828 – and are known as banknotes of the War of the Brothers.

The problem was one of accession to the throne, and it was all extremely complicated with Britain aiding one side. The effect on paper money was that notes were overprinted 'D. MIGUEL I 1828' and others of the same issue, 'D. PEDRO IV 1826'. Even in very tatty condition these notes are acceptable to collectors and to find one in VF condition is extremely rare.

russia

As early as the reign of Peter the Great (1689–1725) Russian authorities considered the possibilities of paper money, but able handling of the economy by the Minister of Finance staved off the necessity for it.

Catherine the Great was to issue paper money some forty years later and examples are known dated 1769. It is possible, however, that paper money was issued in 1762 – a year when Peter III and Catherine the Great both ruled Russia. Evidence for this is based on the personal library of the Minister of War, Potemkin. Volumes, bound in pig-skin, were found to contain pages of 1,000 rouble banknotes. As such a high denomination was not introduced during the issue of Catherine the Great and did not, in fact, become issued until 1886, it is clear that an earlier series of notes was prepared. Russian experts consider that they were distributed, but only to personal friends of the ruler of Russia.

The original decree authorising paper money limited the issue to twenty million roubles. Assignat banks were set up at St Petersburg and Moscow. Issues are known for 1769, 1772, 1773, 1775, 1777, and 1785 consisting of 25, 50, 75 and 100 rouble notes. Then the banks were replaced by ·the Imperial Assignat

Many thousands of different banknotes can be collected from the Soviet Union. They were issued by many different factions during the Revolution etc.

Bank which issued 5, 10, 25, 50 and 100 roubles between 1786 and 1797.

By now the limit placed on issue had been far exceeded, amounting to over 150 million roubles. At the turn of the century Russia's financial situation worsened. Alexander I, Tsar from 1801 to 1825, involved his country in foreign affairs by supplying troops to Britain for the Napoleonic Wars. War with Turkey and

Persia, and then the invasion of Russia by Napoleon, made more and more supplies of paper money necessary. In 1810 a silver rouble was worth four paper money roubles and depreciation was to continue. A Russian statesman, Speransky, attempted to discontinue paper money issues altogether, and revert to silver, but the war did not permit such a move. Speransky was removed from office and D. A. Guriev appointed Minister of Finance. This astute minister managed to reduce the circulating paper money from 836 million to just under 600 million in 1817.

Nicholas I became Tsar of all Russia in 1825 and was perhaps lucky to have the able Minister of Finance, Kankim, who brought stability for a decade. The silver rouble became the standard monetary unit and credit notes replaced the existing paper money by 1843. The Imperial Assignat Bank ceased to function and the State Credit Notes Chancellery took over the note-issue.

Alexander II had little opportunity to right the currency problems because of the Crimean War, which left some 735 million roubles in paper money. The situation worsened in 1877 with the Russo-Turkish war and over 1,150 million paper roubles were circulating. The value of paper roubles fell to 63·2 kopecks.

He issued 1, 3, 5, 10, 25, 50 and 100 rouble notes each year and in 1876 issued 50 and 100 rouble notes which are among the rarer note issues of Russia.

The Populists assassinated Alexander II and Alexander III became Tsar from 1881 to 1894. He managed to stabilize the paper money at 63·2 kopecks, and to combat speculation instituted a special tax of 1 kopeck per 100 roubles. Nicholas II was faced with continual uprisings, the Russo-Japanese War, and World War I, which caused the paper money situation to get out of hand. A bank moratorium was effected freezing all bank accounts of over 100 roubles and allowing people to withdraw only five per cent of their money per month. When the Russian Revolution broke out the Tsar abdicated – 1917 – and was subsequently killed together with his family by the Bolsheviks. A provisional government headed by Prince Lvoff and Kerensky took over the affairs of Russia, ending the rule of the Romanoffs which had lasted over three centuries.

On 2–3 March the Provisional Government came into being.

The nation was in economic distress and the people looked to the new government to produce miracles. Such miracles were not forthcoming. The Bolshevik party, by organising strikes, forced a coalition government – formed by political units of the various factions. Lenin, leading the Bolsheviks, demanded that the Provisional Government should come under the control of the soviets (town councils etc, dominated by the Bolsheviks). On 18 July 1917, General Kornilov moved his forces to Petrograd only to find that some 40,000 of them were for Lenin and ready to fight for Lenin. The military confrontation was cancelled and the government fell.

During its short reign the Kerensky government had inherited financial chaos and resorted to large issues of paper money. By March 1917 the paper rouble was only worth 27 kopecks. It was not within the capability of the Soviet printing works to produce paper money quickly enough and other nations – including the American Bank Note Company – were asked to do the work.

Whereas the Tsarist regime had issued around 270 million roubles a month – the life of paper money was short – this new government was issuing more than 1,000 million roubles a month. Much of the money was on poor quality paper, unsigned and without serial numbers. The people, accustomed to the colourful and intricately designed notes of the Tsars, did not trust the new money. The 'Duma' note for 1,000 roubles was often refused.

Another problem was that the inflationary wage increases brought about the situation that a printer producing small-denomination notes was working at a loss.

Large numbers of 25 and 100 rouble notes were ordered from the United States but as the delivery date could not be before the spring of 1918 the supplies were too late to save the government from collapse.

A 250 rouble note was designed and printed with the double-headed eagle, in an attempt to regain the confidence of the people. On 22 August 1917, 20 and 40 rouble notes were printed, unnumbered and unsigned. The Minister of Finance issued a statement that they were only temporary notes. To save time they were issued in uncut sheets to the banks, whose job it was to cut

One of the 'giant' notes of the last of the Tsars, depicting Peter the Great on the reverse. They were brought out of Russia by the nobility in suitcases, but became worthless. The full area of the note is not shown here

Tsarist plates were often used for Revolutionary issues, and many notes dated 1909 were in fact issued in 1917

them up. This paper money was nicknamed 'beer stamps' by the people.

Although these issues helped the situation, the shortage of small money was such that it became necessary to use postage stamps as currency. Various kopeck denominations were printed on card with an inscription on the back saying that they could pass as money.

The Provisional Government also resorted to using the plates of the old Tsarist paper money. They did so without changing the date or design, and these notes can only be identified by the signatures on the notes.

The next period of paper money in Russia is usually dated between 1917 and 1922 and covers the civil war and the foreign intervention. It is one of the most interesting periods of paper money history in Russia, and much of the paper money is still about and inexpensive. This is more because Westerners cannot understand the Russian text than because of their interest. Indeed the historical struggles they give testimony to are as interesting and worthy of collection as those of any other part of the world.

The West, principally America, Britain and France, not only supplied millions of pounds to the 'white' Russians who evicted the Bolsheviks, but gave limited military assistance. British troops advanced with Russians under General Yudenitch from the north-west. British, American, and French under General Miller came from the north, and in Siberia Americans and Japanese assisted the army of Admiral Kolchak. The Cossacks rode from the south-east, and General Denikin led Romanian, French and Greek troops as well as his own from the south-west. Poles, Germans and Letts marched under General Wrangel. But the Bolsheviks held out.

All these armies needed paper money. The Moscow government made sure its paper money did not reach the White armies, so they had no option but to issue their own money. Some issues are very rare but quite a few were released in huge quantities and are still common. Some hundreds of different notes can be traced. Of particular interest are those issued by Generals Denikin, Chkouro, Wandam, Wrangel, Yudenitch, Diteraides, and Sulkevitch, and by Colonel Avolloff-Bermondt and Admiral Kolchak.

70

To make the position even more complex there were groups who refused to ally themselves with either side. Peoples under the leadership of Ataman Semenoff, Nestor Makhno, issued their own notes.

As with all wars, many cities became cut off from normal supplies, and a host of different types of paper money emerged to combat the situation. Kharkov in the Ukraine issued fifty-six different types of paper money alone, each issue from an organisation like the Chamber of Trade or City notes of France and Germany following the Great War. Even restaurants, trade unions, parent teachers' associations issued paper money. It is believed that nearly 500 Russian cities issued such paper money.

While all this was going on some provinces took advantage of the weakness of the Central Government and established their own governments. The republics of Georgia, Armenia, Turkestan and so on emerged.

Yet another type of paper money was issued in areas occupied by various invading groups. Some of these can be found with Russian and foreign texts, particularly German and Japanese. The Russian Socialist Federation of Soviet Republics now came into being and gradually the insurgent republics were brought to heel. During this period, 1918–23, Tsarist notes were still issued, some of them dated 1909 or 1912–16, even though they were really issued in 1918. Only the signatures can identify them. Bonds bearing interest were also issued and permitted to be used as currency. In this short period well over a hundred different types of paper money came into use.

Then in 1923 the Union of Socialist Soviet Republics – the USSR – was formed. State Bank credit notes including high denominations like 10,000, 15,000 and 25,000 roubles were issued.

Research into Russian paper money will turn up some unusual events. For example, the American-printed notes for the Provisional Government were left in a ship's hold at Vladivostok for some time after the Government had collapsed. Then they were put to use by the White Russians, the 50 kopecks without signature. The government of the Maritime Regions issued some with the signature 'Ivanov' and the government in Baikal overprinted some notes with new denominations.

Banknotes issued by the Hitler regime for the occupation of Russia are among the rarest of all Russian paper money. Indeed only a handful exist and, as far as is known, all are in the possession of the treasury of the USSR.

In denominations of one rouble, one tscherwonez and five tscherwonez, they are believed to have been printed by the State Printing Works in Berlin, but in 1945 the Works were completely destroyed by bombs and no records have been found.

The German paper money specialist Dr Arnold Keller wrote: 'According to the serial numbers they are most certainly printed from our own State Printing Works'. The notes were for issue at the Kiev Bank in 1941. They never went into general circulation.

spain

Claims have been made for a piece of Spanish paper money dated as early as 1250 under King James I of Catalonia and Aragon. Certainly this king founded various banks, but no paper money of that date exists today. When the fortress of Alhama was besieged by the Arabs in 1483, paper money was necessary to pay the soldiers. A similar issue occurred in 1490 during the siege of Granada by the Catholic Kings.

In 1799 King Charles III issued royal securities, and notes for 100, 200, and 1,000 reales are known.

A large issue of *assignats* was made in Spain by the French troops. As the French retreated from Catalonia they proposed changing these Imperial *assignats* – each for 100 pesetas – into silver and gold. But Catalonian patriots ambushed the French convoy bringing the notes from Toulouse and destroyed them. A few survived (and were found at a French command post near Palautrordera), but they are rare.

By 1892 many private banks issued notes in Spain and these notes are also extremely rare because they appear to have been redeemed at all times by the banks.

When the Carlist War broke out early in the nineteenth century, the Duke of Madrid, pretender to the throne, issued notes to pay his troops. The Carlists issued notes paying 25 per cent interest, repayable after two years from the date he took over the throne. Needless to say, they never were redeemed.

Picturesque Spanish Republican issues with historical scenes

The Bank of Spain obtained a monopoly of note issues in 1874. Private banks got round this by issuing bonds bearing interest.

With the outbreak of the Spanish Civil War in 1936 the nation's finances soon took a turn for the worse. Unusually attractive paper money of the Bank of Spain issued for the Republic zone is still obtainable at reasonable prices. Printed by Bradbury, Wilkinson and Co., they show reverse designs of historical scenes and battles.

sweden

The honour of introducing a national banknote currency in Europe goes to Sweden, who introduced such notes in 1661 as a result of reductions in the weight of copper coinage and the resultant shortage. The idea came from Johan Palmstruch, a high-ranking civil servant. In fact Palmstruch had suggested a paper currency as early as 1652 in the form of small bank letters (*Banckbrieflein*).

The first notes were 'credit' notes issued by the Stockholm Bank founded by a Royal Privilege to Palmstruch dated 30 November 1656. These notes were for denominations from 5 to 1,000 copper dalers and Palmstruch himself signed all the notes, which gives them an added attraction to collectors. The notes also bore the signatures of bank staff. Silver daler notes were issued later in 10, 25, 50 and 100 denominations. Some of these notes were signed by no fewer than eleven people!

The notes were intended to be issued to customers of the bank who had deposits and would therefore act as deposit receipts. But in the event the bank issued the notes without such security, causing a situation in 1664 where notes could not be redeemed. The government required the accounts of the bank to be inspected and on finding the true position an order was issued for the immediate arrest of Palmstruch. Subsequently he was sentenced to death, reprieved by the King's favour, and imprisoned.

Although it is difficult to understand how it came about, the Stockholm Bank managed to issue 'transport' notes even after the bankruptcy. These were true deposit receipts.

In 1668 the Swedish Parliament took over the bank and renamed it the Riksens Standers Bank, now known' as Sveriges

Riksbank (the Swedish State Bank) – the oldest national bank in the world.

Smarting under the effects of previous paper issues, Parliament would not permit note issues – despite requests from the bank officials – until 1701.

The history of these notes and subsequent issues is not very inspiring as the bank refused to cash its notes in silver from 1809 until 1830 when the government devalued. From then on the bank's issues grew in stability and in 1873 following the monetary union with Denmark the notes were redeemed in gold. The gold standard was, of course, suspended during World War I – also between 1920 and 1924 – and completely rescinded in 1931.

On occasions in the early banking history of Sweden notes were also issued by state departments and the most interesting of these are the Fahnehielm notes, so named after the civil servant of that name who signed them. These came about during the Swedish-Russian War of 1790 and were valid only in Finland for the payment of goods required by the army.

Private banks were started in 1830 and at first issued notes illegally. From 1904 private banks were forbidden to issue notes and the State took over a complete monopoly of note-issue.

norway

Norway was left in considerable financial plight following the Napoleonic Wars and in 1816 formed the Norges Bank. The silver speciedaler of former times was reinstated as the monetary unit. The first notes of the new bank were issued in 1816 and were on one side of the paper only in black ink. Different watermarks were used for each denomination on paper from the Bentsebrugs Paper Mill.

A new issue of notes was made in 1841, this time on coloured paper and in coloured inks.

In 1866 the whole design was changed again and both sides of the note were now printed on. Modern notes of Norway were introduced in 1877.

6 north america

american colonial paper money

The introduction of paper money to America came about from dire necessity. The British governors of the various territories were under instructions to refuse permission for the Americans to issue paper money of their own unless it was absolutely essential. Consequently the early issues are invariably because of war.

Massachusetts Bay issued notes on 10 December 1690, and these were intended to pay for the military expedition to Canada known as King William's War. South Carolina was next to issue paper money when a military punitive expedition took place against the Spanish and the Indians in Florida. By 1709 New Hampshire, Connecticut, New York and New Jersey had also issued paper money to ease the situation caused by Queen Anne's War (1702–13).

Undoubtedly the restrictions placed on the territories forbidding them to issue paper money hindered the development of the areas. Coin was always in short supply and more and more 'illegal' issues were made.

These early notes are very rough in appearance and are often found with different type faces making up the text of the note. When the Revolution took place the various States made large issues of notes. But it is evident from the notes that not all the States intended that there should be a complete break with Britain. Many issues still referred to the King of England; Georgia even used the Crown as its vignette. Delaware, New Jersey and

76

Early colonial paper money was often issued in defiance of British Law. They are handsigned, often by famous people, and many refer to 'the reign of his Majesty George III'. Both dollars and sterling were in use

Broken bank notes of America

Pennsylvania notes continued to state on the notes 'issued . . . in the reign of King George III' until it became apparent that no reconciliation was possible.

Propaganda quickly replaced these vignettes and notes appeared showing George III trampling on Magna Carta and setting fire to American towns. Famous notes are the 'sword in hand' issues engraved and printed by Paul Revere. They show a Minute Man armed with sword and the words 'Issued in defence of American Liberty'. Another famous issuer of notes was Benjamin Franklin.

Early notes had been in sterling but now the Americans changed to the Spanish dollar.

In 1775 the Continental Congress issued notes. The first issues bore the title 'The United Colonies' but in 1777 it became 'The United States'.

As more and more notes circulated the population became concerned about their redemption, particularly as the British began forging some of the notes on a grand scale with the idea of ruining an already tottering economy (an idea which the Germans tried on the British in 1939–45!). To make the notes acceptable the practice grew up of having the most respected and esteemed people hand-sign them. Because of this autograph-hunters as well as paper money collectors are always on the lookout for early American colonial money. Nine signatories of the Declaration of Independence can be found on paper money, as well as seven signatories of the Articles of Confederation, ten of the Stamp Act Congress and eleven of the United States Constitution. Most of the signatories of the notes – and there were often several to a note – can be traced in American history as men who took a leading part in the affairs of the nation.

Fortunately for collectors, the known issues of Colonial America have all been thoroughly catalogued by Eric P. Newman in his book *The Early Paper Money of America.*

broken bank notes

After the successful conclusion of the American War of Independence the Government as such took no further interest in paper money, preferring to put its trust in gold and silver. However, it

Small denomination notes were issued by County banks

did nothing effective to stop private banks. As early as 1791 – 1836 the First and Second Banks of the United States did their best to control issues but by 1836 the private banks of the various States had virtually taken over the banking system.

These private bank notes are extremely colourful and tell the history of the growth of America. Scenes show mining, hunting, Indians, ships, cowboys and just about every facet of American life at that time.

In the mid-nineteenth century there were no restrictions on note issues and the result was that in the years 1837, 1841 and 1857 there were tremendous failures which brought about misery and suffering to note-holders. Even so new banks sprang up with ever more colourful notes. By the start of the Civil War it is known that some 1,600 banks had issued their own notes and over 10,000 different types of notes were in existence. Also, something like 5,000 contemporary forgeries were in existence! Whereas it is often virtually impossible to find United States notes in crisp condition, a great many of the broken bank notes are found crisp because they did not circulate to any extent before they became irredeemable. Indeed they get their name 'broken bank notes' from the fact that with hardly any exceptions they all went bankrupt. The best reference work for these notes is *North American Currency* by Grover C. Criswell which devotes some 800 pages to the notes (the book deals with other currencies as well) and does not pretend to be complete.

Of all the American paper money issues these are the most attractive and the least expensive to collectors.

confederate paper money

All United States paper money is valid and the first issues of 1861 are extremely rare. But this is not so of the Confederate states whose contemporary issues were to become unredeemable at the end of the war. Confederate states were in an even worse financial plight than the United States when hostilities commenced. To offset this they issued millions of dollars' worth of paper money.

Confederate notes can be divided into those of the Confederate States of America and those of the individual states. Early issues include a 1000 dollar note showing John C. Calhoun (left) and Andrew Jackson (right), which is probably the rarest issue of all the Confederate paper money. Many of the $100 notes carry the wording 'interest at Two Cents Per Day'.

The most common issue was the last one made in 1864. A Confederate Act of 17 February 1864 authorised $200 million but it is believed that something like ten times that amount was actually printed. Collectors have found hundreds of varieties in this series and while most are common there are some great rarities to be found. One note which has always been popular with collectors is the $500 note of 1864 which depicts General 'Stonewall' Jackson together with the Confederate flag and arms.

There was a shortage of paper in the Confederacy and some notes have been found printed on brown wrapping paper and a wide variety of watermarked paper. Keenly sought after are the pink 50 cent notes printed on paper sent out from Britain in ships which successfully breached the United States blockade.

Most Confederate notes have blank reverses and these were used for interest payment stamps, etc. Often badly printed, they were also forged in vast quantities and, to make matters worse, modern forgeries have also been made. At one stage a chewing gum manufacturer gave away imitation Confederate notes, and these often turn up offered as genuine notes! They are easy to detect as they are much smaller than the genuine notes and the signatures are printed, while Confederate notes were hand-signed.

Even now much research is needed into the issues of the

Confederate states though many thousands have been catalogued by Grover C. Criswell and Clarence L. Criswell in their book *Confederate and Southern State Currency*, which is the standard reference work on these issues.

At the end of the war the United States refused to redeem Confederate currency at all and great hardship was caused. Soldiers would stuff their boots with hundred dollar bills simply to keep their feet warm.

For many years they fetched little as collector's pieces but today they are in demand. They bear testimony to a great historical event and though it is possible to buy many of the higher denominations at well below face it has been forecast that the time will come when a $100 Confederate bill will be worth $100.

the united states

When Lincoln became President of the United States in 1861 the Treasury was in trouble and government securities were well below par. The national debt was more than 76 million dollars and with the threat of civil war paper money issues became essential. The suspension of specie payment at the outbreak of war caused postage stamps to circulate as currency. John Gault of Boston, finding that stamps quickly became dirty and torn when used as currency, invented a special metal case with a thin mica cover over the front of the stamp. Gault was granted a patent on 12 August 1862 for the 'postage stamp case' and was soon selling advertisement space on the back of the cases.

The demand for these encased postage stamps was such that many post offices even in large cities were selling out of stamps. The Government refused to let Gault have supplies once it became clear that the operation was on a tremendous scale. The Treasury came to the public rescue by replacing the encased postage stamps with postage currency. These were small notes with designs of postage stamps on them, representing the value of the note. The first issue was even perforated like stamps. Before long the postage currency was replaced by fractional currency notes.

Collectors should remember that all notes issued by the United States Government are still valid today, and many people do not realise that 3 cent notes exist!

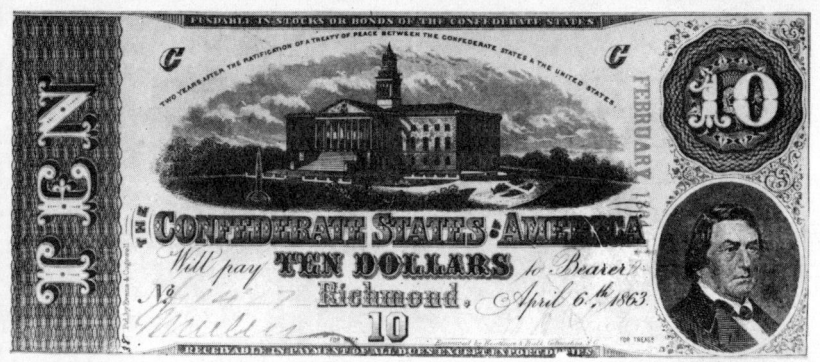

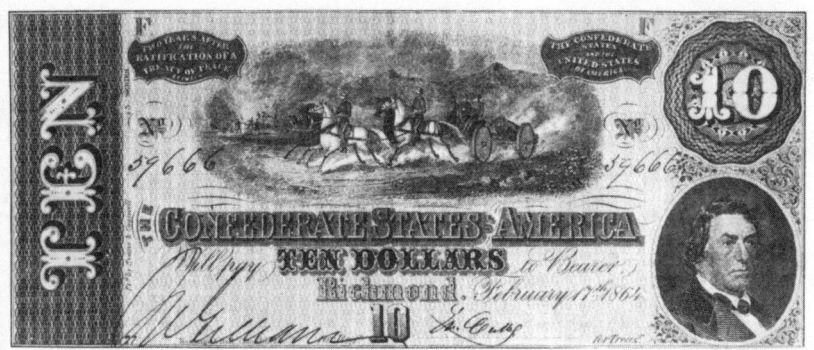

Confederate notes which became worthless at the end of the war and were used by soldiers to stuff in their boots to keep their feet warm. The $10 1864 issue shows a southern horse artillery gun being brought into action

Fractional currency of the USA

In large cities the practice also grew up of putting stamps in little envelopes to be passed as money and fairly soon specially printed envelopes, at least thirteen different types, were in use.

The postage and fractional issues were printed in various issues and types, so much so that many collectors specialise just in these issues and their many varieties.

Twelve major types of currency notes have been issued by the United States since 1861, apart from the postage currency. The United States were fortunate in having as their first secretary of the Treasury, Salmon Portland Chase. But even though he was against issues of paper money he had to tell Congress that the situation was so bad that paper money was the only solution. On 17 July 1861, Congress passed an Act enabling Chase to produce paper money in the form of Treasury notes and bonds.

Extremely rare are the first few of these notes, for it was the practice to hand-sign paper money, and General Spinner, as Treasurer of the United States, started signing notes. He very quickly decided it was not practical to hand-sign notes on the scale now required and formed a team of men to do the work, requiring them to write in 'for the' by the side of 'Treasurer of the United States'. These notes are also great rarities, as the next issue had the words 'for the' set in type. Demand notes were issued without the Treasury seal and are the only United States notes without the seal. All of them are rare.

It was the demand notes which gave rise to the term 'greenback'.

Legal tender notes, also known as United States notes, were first issued on 10 March 1862 in denominations of 5 to 1,000 dollars. They get their name from the obligation printed on the note: 'This note is a legal tender for all debts, public and private, except duties on imports and interest on the public debt, and is exchangeable for US six per cent twenty year bonds, redeemable at the pleasure of the United States after five years'. The obligation was changed in subsequent issues. Altogether there were five separate issues of these notes.

Compound Interest Treasury notes were authorised in 1863 and were an attempt to help the nation's finances which were in a terrible state owing to the Civil War. Denominations of 10, 20, 50, 100, 500 and 1000 dollars were issued. The $10 shows the head of Salmon Portland Chase. They bore interest of six per cent compounded every six months, but were payable only at the end of three years, and the notes were known as 'three year treasury notes'.

Interest-bearing notes are the rarest of all the United States issues. Notes were issued for one year, two years and three years. One year notes carried five per cent interest which was payable at the end of the year when the note could be presented. The three year notes are exceptional in that they had five coupons attached to them for the payment of interest. Interest was paid every six months so a coupon was taken off on each interest payment being made except the last when the actual note was redeemed. All these interest-bearing notes are of the greatest rarity among collectors and only two notes are known which still contain the five coupons.

Another unusual type of paper money was the refunding certificate. This came about as the result of an Act of Congress on 26 February 1879 and the idea was to get the ordinary citizen to invest money with the government. The notes were for $10 and bore interest of four per cent per year. Originally it was intended to let the notes accrue in value indefinitely, but when the interest value of the notes alone had exceeded the value of the notes – they reached $11·30 in interest, making the notes worth more than double face – the payment of interest was stopped (1 July 1907). Two types were issued, both showing the head of Benjamin Franklin.

Silver certificates were authorised by Acts of Congress made in 1878 and 1880 and bear blue seals. Congress stopped the issues of silver certificates on 4 June 1963, but a lot were presumably in existence, as the Secretary of the Treasury stopped the outflow of silver dollars, saying that the silver bullion was needed to redeem silver certificates.

The very first issue of silver certificates was in denominations of 10 to 1000 dollars but the second issue introduced lower denominations starting at one dollar. One of the most attractive series of all US paper money is that known as the educational set. These were the third issue of silver certificates, made up of 1, 2 and 5 dollar notes in 1896. A wide variety of signature combinations exists on these notes and many collectors specialise in silver certificates.

Treasury or coin notes were issued in 1890 for the purpose of paying for silver bullion which had the effect that they were fully backed by metal coin. The notes were redeemed in gold or silver until recent years when they have only been paid out in silver. The Treasury Department has set aside the necessary amount of silver to redeem all outstanding coin notes.

The Californian Gold Rush saw an issue of national gold bank notes of California. Printed on yellow paper, they depict gold coins according to the denomination of the notes. It was found more convenient to use paper money rather than continually weigh gold coin when doing business so these notes were issued by Act of Congress in 1870 to facilitate trade. They were redeemable in actual gold and were quickly accepted by the Californian population. They are all rare and none are known in perfect condition.

Another interesting issue of notes is the gold certificates which were printed in a gold colour; in all, nine different issues were made. Some of these were printed on one side of the paper only, and it seems that the first few issues were used mainly for accountancy purposes in the banks. But the fourth issue, dated 1882, went into general circulation with denominations of $20 to $10,000. The last issue was made between 1913 and 1922.

Thousands of banks throughout the United States issued national bank notes between 1863 and 1929. Charters were granted to banks allowing them to issue notes of their own up to the value of 90 per cent of the securities deposited with the government. This meant, of course, that the issue was fully backed. Charters were granted for twenty year periods and then needed renewal. Collectors endeavour to find the different signature combinations or to collect those of a particular state or city. The first charter period saw notes which are among the most beautiful in the world and the vignettes unfold the story of American progress and history.

The series of 1882, or the second charter period, saw the 'brownbacks' and many new banks obtained charters. Several different designs were used during the series and later ones became conventional greenbacks.

A complete change of designs for all denominations was made for the third charter period which notes bear the series date of 1902.

With the introduction of the Federal Reserve system Federal Reserve bank notes were issued and inscribed 'national currency'. Two distinctive types of issue were made, the series of 1915 and the series of 1918. There were twelve banks which formed the system, but the first series only has notes from Atlanta, Chicago, Kansas City, Dallas and San Francisco. It is to be noted that the obligation to pay was not that of the United States but only that of the Federal Reserve Bank.

It is believed that nearly 800 million dollars were issued in Federal Reserve bank notes and that now less than two million have not been redeemed.

The Federal Reserve Act of 23 December 1913 also permitted Federal Reserve notes. These notes differ from the Federal Reserve Bank notes in that the former were issued by the United States and sent to the twelve Federal Reserve Banks whose job it was then to spread them through the banking system. The Federal Reserve notes carried the obligation of the government of the United States and not that of the Bank.

Modern United States small currency notes were introduced into circulation on 10 July 1929, though some carry the date 1928. They form one of the most popular types of collection in the United States as there are literally hundreds of different notes which can go to make up such a collection. While, of course, the high denominations are beyond the reach of the average collector, nevertheless an extremely interesting collection can be made of the low denominations, particularly the dollar bill. Two thirds of all USA bills are one dollar denominations.

The reason the small-size notes replaced the old familiar large 'greenbacks' used since the Civil War is rather unusual. Dr Meredith of the Bureau of Engraving and Printing had sent designs for the proposed Philippine paper money in 1903. They were accepted but the Secretary of War, Elihu Root, was concerned that the paper money would be confused with the United States notes. For that reason it was decided to print the Philippine money in a smaller size.

Then, in 1910, Secretary MacVeagh recommended that the United States should change their size to that of the Philippine size which had been a tremendous success. He pointed out that there would be considerable savings because of the saving of paper and the ability to increase the rate of production etc. He estimated that in the year 1910 the saving would amount to over $612,000! Administrative processes delayed the matter until 26 February 1913 when Mr MacVeagh gave formal instructions to the Bureau to proceed to print 'to the dimensions of the Philippine certificates'.

It would seem that the small-size currency was certain to appear in that year but, as it happened, Mr MacVeagh retired within a week of giving the instruction and the new secretary, Mr McAdoo, decided to postpone the matter while he settled into his new office. The advent of World War I shelved the whole idea and it was not until 1922 that serious consideration was again given to small-size notes when President Harding wrote to the secretary:

'Personally I have long since been inclined to favour the smaller-sized bill'.

The wheels of officialdom slowly started again and by 1925 the General Currency Committee voted unanimously to reduce the paper size. Finally they appeared on 10 July 1929.

The collector will quickly learn that regardless of the 'type' of note, those of the same denomination always bear the same portrait. There are twelve denominations but the highest, the hundred thousand dollar note, was only used for internal accountancy in the Federal Reserve Banks and was never issued to the public for general circulation.

The notes are:

One dollar	George Washington
Two dollars	Thomas Jefferson
Five dollars	Abraham Lincoln
Ten dollars	Alexander Hamilton
Twenty dollars	Andrew Jackson
Fifty dollars	Ulysses S. Grant
100 dollars	Benjamin Franklin
500 dollars	William McKinley
1000 dollars	Grover Cleveland
5000 dollars	James Madison
10,000 dollars	Salmon P. Chase
100,000 dollars	Woodrow Wilson

There are six types of note:

United States note
silver certificate
national currency
Federal Reserve Banknote
Federal Reserve note
gold certificate

They are easily identified, as they bear those names. United States notes were introduced by Act of Congress in 1862. The smaller sized notes dated 1928 are obsolete and the two dollar notes were stopped in July 1965 – they had for some time been considered 'unlucky' by the public. The $5 was discontinued in

1967. In 1966, however, a $100 bill was released. A tight rein is kept on the number of these notes outstanding and nearly half of the amount is backed by gold. All such notes bear a red seal.

Silver certificates were abolished in June 1963 and redemption in silver ceased on 24 June 1968. But from 1878 when first introduced (small sized were issued first in 1929 and dated 1928) until that time they could be surrendered against silver. The first modern issue had the words 'One Silver Dollar payable to the bearer on demand'. In 1934 this was changed to 'one Dollar in silver payable to the bearer on demand', which had the important effect of allowing the Treasury to redeem them against any standard silver coin or bullion. An important exception to this was the ten dollar bill of 1933 series with the words 'Ten dollars payable in silver coin'. Perhaps one of the rarest of modern USA notes is the Julian-Woodin signatures, only 216,000 were printed – a minute delivery for modern USA notes – and are catalogued as high as $450 by collectors. Those with the Julian-Morgenthau signatures are even rarer (though 336,000 were printed) as most were destroyed by the Treasury.

National currency notes were permitted by an Act of 1863, superseded by another Act of 3 June 1864, which allowed national banks to be set up and to issue notes against securities lodged with the Treasury. The issue of these notes ceased in 1935. They bear the wording: 'Redeemable in Lawful Money of the United States at United States Treasury or at the Bank of Issue'. The names of the banks, cities and states appear on these notes and provide a formidable task for completion – there are notes from 51 states available with a great many more city names and bank names. They have brown seals.

The Federal Reserve System was established in 1913 and today forms the main currency note issue of the United States – something like 90 per cent of all notes are Federal Reserve notes. In denominations of $1 to $10,000 they were first issued in small-size in 1929, dated 1928, though in 1946 notes of $5000 and above were no longer printed. The twelve Federal Reserve Banks are supervised by a Board of Governors of the Federal Reserve System which is appointed by the President of the United States. The big twelve are: Boston, New York, Philadelphia, Cleveland,

Richmond, Atlanta, Chicago, St. Louis, Minneapolis, Kansas City, Dallas and San Francisco. The bank seal on the left of the obverse of the note gives the name of the particular bank. These notes have green seals.

Small-sized Federal Reserve bank notes were first issued in 1933 as an emergency measure to counter heavy withdrawals of Federal Reserve notes in that year. In fact the plates of the national currency notes were adapted and the year series date of 1929 was not altered. While still headed 'national currency' the overprinting on the left now read 'The Federal Reserve Bank of ...' instead of 'The ... National Bank ...' They were discontinued in 1935 and, in mint condition, are probably much scarcer than current prices would indicate. As against the Federal Reserve notes, these were not obligations of the United States but of the individual Federal Reserve Banks. Like the national currency notes, they bear brown seals.

Then there are the gold certificates which by an Act of 1933 had to be presented and changed for other currency. That many people disregarded the order was evidenced by the action of Treasury Secretary Dillon in 1964. He rescinded the order to the extent that the public were permitted possession of gold certificates issued before the Gold Reserve Act of 1934 which had raised the value of gold, made gold coin illegal, and permitted gold certificates to be issued for internal circulation to Federal Reserve Banks only. The effect of the 1964 order was to permit collectors to display gold certificates!

The collector also finds that there are a fair number of signature combinations to be found on the various types of notes of the United States.

They are:

H. T. Tate – A. W. Mellon
W. O. Woods – A. W. Mellon
W. O. Woods – Ogden L. Mills
W. O. Woods – W. H. Woodin
W. A. Julian – W. H. Woodin
W. A. Julian – Henry Morgenthau Jr.
W. A. Julian – Fred M. Vinson

W. A. Julian – John W. Snyder
Georgia Neese Clark – John W. Snyder
Ivy Baker Priest – G. M. Humphrey
Ivy Baker Priest – Robert B. Anderson
Elizabeth Rudel Smith – C. Douglas Dillon
Kathryn O'Hay Granahan – C. Douglas Dillon
Kathryn O'Hay Granahan – Henry H. Fowler
Kathryn O'Hay Granahan – Joseph W. Barr
E. E. Jones – W. O. Woods.

When a slight change to a note was needed such as a change of Treasurer or Secretary needing a new signature it became the practice to add a letter after the series year. Thus, notes of the 1928 series for $2 can be found: 1928, 1928A, 1928B, 1928C, 1928D, 1928E, 1928F, 1928G.

It is also possible to obtain uncut sheets. Current notes are printed in sheets of 12 but sheets of 18 and 32 have been printed. Serial and plate numberings make it possible to reconstruct sheets.

Special issues were made during World War II. In case Japan should succeed in invading Hawaii notes for use in Hawaii were clearly overprinted on the front and back with the name 'Hawaii'. The idea was that if the invasion took place such notes could quickly be declared invalid without interfering with normal United States paper money.

Some notes of the war period are found with the letter 'R' or 'S' by the right hand seal. These were in connection with experiments for paper quality (the average life of a dollar is eighteen months) but nothing came of them as the regular paper continued in use.

Since 1957 the national motto was gradually introduced on notes and today all US currency bears the motto: 'In God We Trust'.

Collectors of modern United States currency will also be interested in military payment certificates. They are issued in denominations of 5 cents to $20 and are for the use only of military personnel overseas. First issued in 1946, they are subject to abrupt changes of type and to the old notes being declared invalid. Twelve different issues have been made so far, depicting attractive girls' heads.

canada

Paper money was introduced as early as 1685 in Canada, and it came in a most unusual form. Jacques de Meulles, Intendant of New France, was unable to pay the troops in coin and in desperation made paper money out of playing cards. It seems that playing cards were the only paper considered suitable for use as money at that time. The date and denomination were written on the back and the cards were signed by the Governor and the Intendant, and countersigned by the Clerk of the Treasury as they were issued.

Large denominations were made on whole cards, smaller denominations on quarters and halves. They were redeemed within a year (and the retention of playing card money after redemption date was punishable by death). The economic situation did not improve and altogether eight such issues were made. Later issues were made on plain white cardboard. It is not thought that any of the early issues exist (forgeries are about) but the Bank of Canada has some sixteen different types of card money in its collection. When the battle of Quebec put an end to French sovereignty over Canada the French Government refused to honour their outstanding card money issues and the British Government finally authorised money to redeem many of them at twenty-five per cent of face.

Until the introduction of decimal currency in Canada in 1858, the British Government virtually ignored the currency needs of this great dominion. So private citizens produced their own paper money. The earliest known notes are those of George King, Quebec City, in 1772 for 3, 6, 12, 15, 20 and 24 coppers.

The earliest known bankers, Dobie and Badgley, issued notes in Montreal in sols and livres in 1790.

The War of 1812–15 put the British in financial difficulties and special Army Bills were issued from the Treasury Office in Quebec for the payment of troops.

Canadian card money had made people distrustful of paper money, but the full redemption of the Army Bills at the end of the war paved the way for the first successful bank in 1817. This was the Montreal Bank which opened in November of that year (it

Early card money of Canada

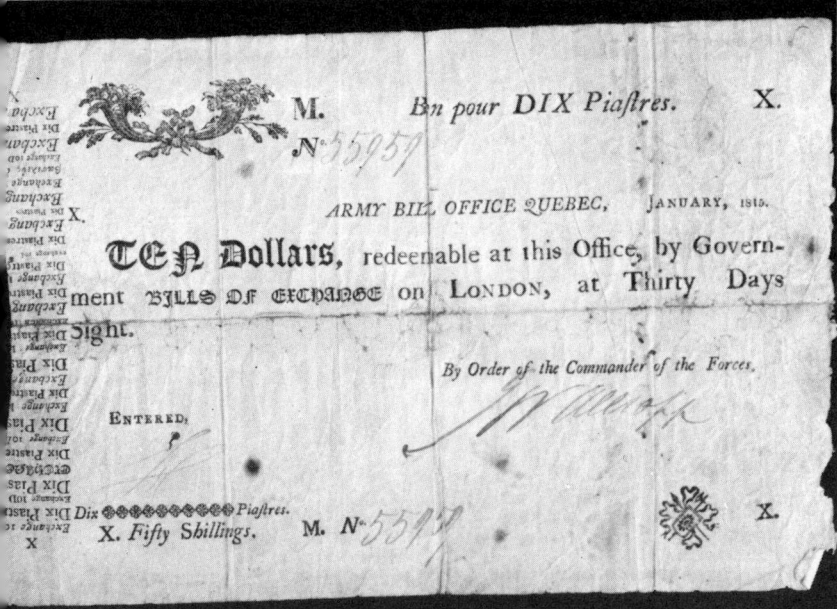

An army bill of Quebec dated 1815

changed its name to the Bank of Montreal in 1822), and was soon followed by the pioneer banking firms of the Quebec Bank, Bank of Canada, Bank of New Brunswick, and the Bank of Upper Canada, York, Bank of Upper Canada, Kingston, and the Halifax Banking Company.

In the nineteenth century over a hundred note-issuing banks were established, and their notes can form a superb collection, involving as they do different currencies and highly colourful and imaginative designs. Until about 1840 all these notes had a design only on one side of the note. Some notes were in sterling and others in both sterling and dollars. At that time there was no Canadian dollar and the dollars could be American or Spanish (Spanish dollars were legal tender in Canada until 1860). Sterling notes did not necessarily refer to British currency, but sometimes to Halifax or York which both had different systems. Notes can be found using only the English language, only the French language, and bi-lingual.

One way of collecting paper money is to get as many different denominations as possible – and Canada provides a field-day. Until about 1860 $3 notes were quite common as were $4 notes. Some banks issued notes for $6 and Molson's Bank made an issue of a $7 note in 1871. Notes for $8 and $25 also exist.

At the same time the Government issued its own treasury notes in certain areas: the island of Saint John (now Prince Edward Island), Nova Scotia (1812), Newfoundland (1834). The Province of Canada made an issue in 1866 including a high denomination of $500.

But the shortage of small change remained acute and merchants issued small denomination notes for 5, 10, 25 and 50 cents. They were known often as 'bons' and in some cases became the established monetary system – as with the notes of the Hudson's Bay Company which were almost the only currency used in the far north from 1820 to 1870.

By this time just about every conceivable type of currency was doing duty in Canada from wampum beads to bons, but in 1870 the first steps were taken to put Canada's currency on a standard footing. The Government bought up American coins and shipped them back to America, introducing their own. Foreign coins were declared no longer legal tender. Because it was not possible to introduce enough silver to make up the deficiency thus caused, the Government issued 25 cent notes as a temporary expedient. These 'shin-plasters' were soon popular and, taking advantage of their popularity, the Government kept them going until 1935. Designs were changed in 1900 and 1923 and both these last two issues have tiny numbers on them indicating the plate they were printed from. In its enormous collection of paper money the Bank of Canada has over 300 plate numbers on these notes.

The first Bank of Canada notes went into circulation in 1935. Paper money known as 'bank legals' had previously been used by the Dominion of Canada banking system, first appearing in 1896 in denominations of $500, $1000 and $5,000. But they were only for internal transfers and were never available to the public. The highest denomination 'bank legal' was for $50,000 – issued in both 1918 and 1924. These were discontinued with the emergence of the Bank of Canada.

Private banks gradually disappeared through failures, liquida-

Specimen $5 Canadian note showing lumberjacks

Private bank issues of Canada

Devil's head and re-issue without devil's head

tions and amalgamations and much research is still needed to trace them and their histories. Over two thousand different notes of private banks are known in Canada and the probability is that more will turn up. Some, like the Farmers Bank of St John and the Bank of Charlottetown, remain a mystery – testimony to their existence being confined solely to the little pieces of paper issued.

During the depression of the 1930s special 'depression Scrip' was issued, and in World War II prisoner of war money redeemable in camp canteens was introduced for the German prisoners sent to Canada.

Among the modern paper money is an interesting oddity. The design of the Queen's head showed an unmistakable 'Devil's head' in her hair. Whatever the reason for its presence in the design, the authorities thought it advisable to re-engrave the plates, and subsequent issues of Queen Elizabeth II had the 'Devil's head' removed.

7 south and central america

With the exception of Mexico little is known about the early notes of many Central and South American nations. The research worker has much to do in this field and the research can be rewarding for some of the historical events behind early notes are quite extraordinary. Certainly they can match the interest of the issues of Europe and North America.

argentina

A unique turn of events was caused by the issue of notes of the London and River Plate Bank in Argentina. It resulted in the despatch of a British gunboat to Rosario – and an immediate volte-face by the Argentinians. It was the culmination of a series of crises. The tried and proven British bankers' methods had proved too good for the native banks and they attempted to liquidate the bank which they regarded as a menace to the government of the day.

The London Bank was founded in 1862 and the first manager, Mr J. H. Green, sailed across to Argentina in October of that year with two heavy cases full of gold doubloons, letters of credit and account books. Branches were opened in Buenos Aires and Montevideo. Early in 1863 notes were issued, dated for 1862. A commercial crisis saw the bank extended to its full measure of reserves almost immediately but nevertheless it survived and quickly prospered.

In 1866 a branch was opened at Rosario in anticipation of the opening up of large tracts of land between Rosario and Cordoba with the extension of the railways.

The Banco Nacional and the Banco de la Provincia de Santa Fe operating in the area were unable to compete successfully against the 'foreign' bank.

The latter bank was basically owned by the provincial government which decided to use ruthless methods to destroy the London and River Plate Bank. First it forbade the payment of these notes in Bolivian silver and required that notes were to be redeemed in pesos of gold. The London bank did not contest this move and continued to thrive. By 1874 its deposits were four times greater than those of the other banks.

When the amount of business forced the London Bank to present banknotes to the Banco de la Provincia for redemption this was too much for the provincial government. Among the steps it took was the issue of a decree withdrawing the right to issue notes from all banks except the Banco Nacional and the Banco de la Provincia. For good measure it slapped a heavy tax on all banks – except its own – operating in the area of Santa Fe.

The London Bank struck back by suing the government at Federal Court and petitioning the Santa Fe president, Nicolas Avallaneda. Negotiations began to amalgamate the bank with the Banco Provincial – a proposal which received an outright rejection by the London Bank. In May 1876 the provincial government ordered the compulsory liquidation of the Bank of London and River Plate. It openly declared that the bank was a menace to the province's credit.

The manager, Mr Ludwig Behn, fought against this and a petition was organised, supporting the bank. By this time the Banco Provincial was in trouble and coveted the sizeable gold reserves of the London Bank. Literally the day after the government agreed to withdraw the decree of liquidation if the bank agreed to loan money to them, police broke into the London Bank.

Mr Behn was taken completely by surprise and was ordered to liquidate the bank immediately. He was then instructed to deliver all the gold to the Banco Provincial. He refused, was arrested, and the gold was removed by force. Mr Behn was thrown into prison.

When the British Minister in Buenos Aires, Sir Spenser St

John, heard of this he ordered a gunboat to sail from Montevideo for Rosario with all speed.

The Santa Fe foreign minister, Irigoyen, found himself confronted with British guns and hastily agreed to guarantee the bank's property and to release the bank manager if the gunboat was withdrawn.

The German Minister – who represented Mr Behn as one of his nationals – wrote: 'The whole affair presents a series of illegitimate and violent acts which ought not to have been possible in a country that considers itself entitled to claim a place among modern civilised states...'

Soon after that the chairman of the London Bank, George W. Drabble, arrived in Argentina and decided to close the branch. But the government was obliged to withdraw the liquidation order on the London Bank as such because it badly needed a loan from it!

Ten years later internal chaos led to the collapse of most private banks. Only two survived, the London and River Plate Bank and the Banco Comercial. By 1885 the drain on the nation's gold and silver caused the country to go over to paper money completely. The London and River Plate Bank amalgamated with the London and Brazilian Bank under the name of the Bank of London and South America in 1923. Today it is the only British bank in Argentina.

brazil

For more than 150 years Brazil has issued a wide variety of types of paper money, much of it still unclassified. As a Portuguese colony (until 1815) drafts were issued by the Royal Diamond Administration, which was a monopoly of the Crown, for the payment of prospectors. These notes were really just forms filled in by hand for the value of the gold or precious stones deposited by the prospectors. These forms could be exchanged for coin but were soon circulating as money.

Legally issued notes started in 1833 with the Treasury issues (on the notes they are headed 'Thesouro' or 'Tesouro') of Perkins, Bacon of London. Later empire notes were printed by Bradbury Wilkinson in milreis denominations. When the Republic was declared the design of these notes was continued but the legend was changed from 'Imperio do Brasil' to 'Republica dos Estados Unidos do Brasil'. The vignette of Dom Pedro was taken off. These were printed by the American Banknote Company.

During the empire and the republic, private banks were permitted to issue notes. The earliest known bank to issue its private notes was the Bank of Brazil in 1810. This was liquidated in 1829 and the present Bank of Brazil opened in 1853.

Forgery of copper coin in the empire became so widespread that the government admitted that more than half the copper in circulation was forged. To combat the situation the copper coinage was called in. The coins themselves were overstamped for half their original value and in 1833 special Troco de Cobre (Copper Exchange notes) were issued.

A considerable number of revolutionary and semi-official notes were also issued in Brazil. The Republic of Piratini set up in the Farroupilha War of 1845 issued notes, as did revolutionaries of Rio Grande do Sul in 1924 and São Paulo in 1932. Some of the States in Brazil have issued paper money in the form of *apolices,* interest-bearing bonds allowed to circulate as money. This happened as late as 1956 in Rio Grande do Sul. The notes were called brizzolettas after the Governor, Leonel Brizzola, who had caused the illegal issue.

Current notes of Brazil are in cruzeiro denominations and, owing to the habit of the government of devaluing its money as often as two or three times a year, they are among the cheapest circulating notes that collectors can obtain. Some of them literally have a face value of 2d. Highly colourful, they depict battle scenes and other subjects on the reverses.

cuba

Cuba has produced some really beautiful banknotes in its early history, notes being printed by American Banknote Co., National Banknote Co., and Bradbury Wilkinson and Co. Early in the sixteenth century Cuba came under Spanish control and for centuries coins sufficed for the island's needs. But, ravaged by insurgents, the Spanish in 1872 resorted to paper money to combat the 1869 revolution, which was to last for ten years. The notes depict historical figures and events, the island's pro-

Cuban counterfoil issue ·

duce etc. The Queen of Spain appears on the 1 peso note of 1896.

At first all issues were redeemable in gold and enjoyed the trust of the people. But in 1896 the Commander of the Spanish forces, General Valeriano Weler, forced into circulation an issue of 30 million pesos. This over-issue led to inflation, and in an attempt to avert disaster the notes were overprinted PLATA (silver) in red. Eight main issues of notes were made under Spanish rule. Under the Castro regime, Cuba has issued some very distinctive notes depicting marching soldiers and military scenes.

costa rica

In the year that Costa Rica left the United Provinces of Central America it issued its first paper money in denominations of 1, 5, and 10 pesos. These were known as 'Vales' and were bonds or promissory notes. In 1843 these notes were re-issued surcharged for 10 per cent. These issues were, however, so small that much foreign currency was used in the country and the government decided to introduce a national currency. This was done in 1846. A decree passed in 1849 authorised 25,000 pesos in Billetes Nacionales, but within a year of their circulation they had to be withdrawn, owing to successful forging, verified and stamped for re-issue. Further issues were made in 1854 and 1856.

A new type of paper was introduced in 1865 in an attempt to beat forgery. This was 'papier en transparent', each denomination being distinctively coloured.

103

Mexico issued hundreds of pictorial notes in the early twentieth century

The first large bank to be founded was the Banco Anglo-Costarricense whose notes, issued in 1866, were widely accepted. In 1867 the government formed the Banco Nacional de Costa Rica and its first issue consisted of the old stock of Billetes Nacionales overprinted.

The national bank failed in 1877 and was replaced by the Banco de Emisión which now used old stocks of the first national bank stamped and countersigned on the reverse by the Minister of Finance.

This second national bank was also liquidated, in 1884, and succeeded by the Banco de la Unión. In 1900 this bank changed its name to the Bank of Costa Rica.

At one stage certificates of Public Debt were permitted as legal tender and in 1885 the normal treasury emission of $600,000 pesos was set aside to allow another 500,000 pesos to be issued because of the war with Guatemala. This is known as the Emisión de Guerra.

The currency reform of 1896 reintroduced the gold standard and renamed the currency 'colon(es)'.

In July 1902 Certificados de Plata were issued in denominations of 1 and 2 colones. These were backed by 100 per cent silver.

The Banco Anglo-Costarricense also made an issue in 1902 of 100 colones notes using old notes of its own bank overprinted with the new date.

While for a time Costa Rica's finances seemed in good order the violent earthquake of 1910 and World War I brought about a situation where notes were inconvertible. In February 1915 the Banco Commercial went bankrupt with over 800,000 colones in circulation. The government took over the discharge of the notes to avoid the economic downfall the event threatened.

In the years that followed inflation swept the country and large issues were made. The 1000 colones (2,5000,000 printed) were called 'bedsheets' because of their unusually large size. The government was replaced in 1918 and the new congress undertook to stabilise its finances with some international assistance. This resulted in a new issue of Billetes de Plata.

Costa Rican finances have never been really stable, however, and today their paper money is better known to collectors for its beautiful colouring and attractive designs than for its economic stability.

mexico

Cattle thief, bandit and Robin Hood to the poor Mexicans, Doroteo Arango (better known to the world as Pancho Villa) rose to the title of General Francisco Villa in the bloody revolutions of his country and issued paper money bearing his name.

Villa was prompted to join Francisco Madero to overthrow President Diaz in 1910 by the size of the reward the government was prepared to pay for Villa dead or alive. Madero's presidency was cut short by assassination in 1913 and Villa now joined with Carranza to drive General Huerta's army out of the country.

He fell out with Carranza, and when the United States supported Carranza, Villa caused Americans to be slaughtered. General John J. Pershing led an expedition into Mexico to capture Villa but failed. But Carranza's army forced him out of Mexico City.

In 1923 Pancho Villa was shot dead while being driven to a meeting.

The Tesoreria General del Estado de Chihuahua paper issue of 10 December 1913 shows Villa's name as provisional governor. Denominations of 5, 10, 25, 50 centavos and 1, 2, 5, 10, 20, 50, 100 pesos were issued.

Numerous varieties occur as such notes were often stamped 'Revalidated' to check counterfeiting.

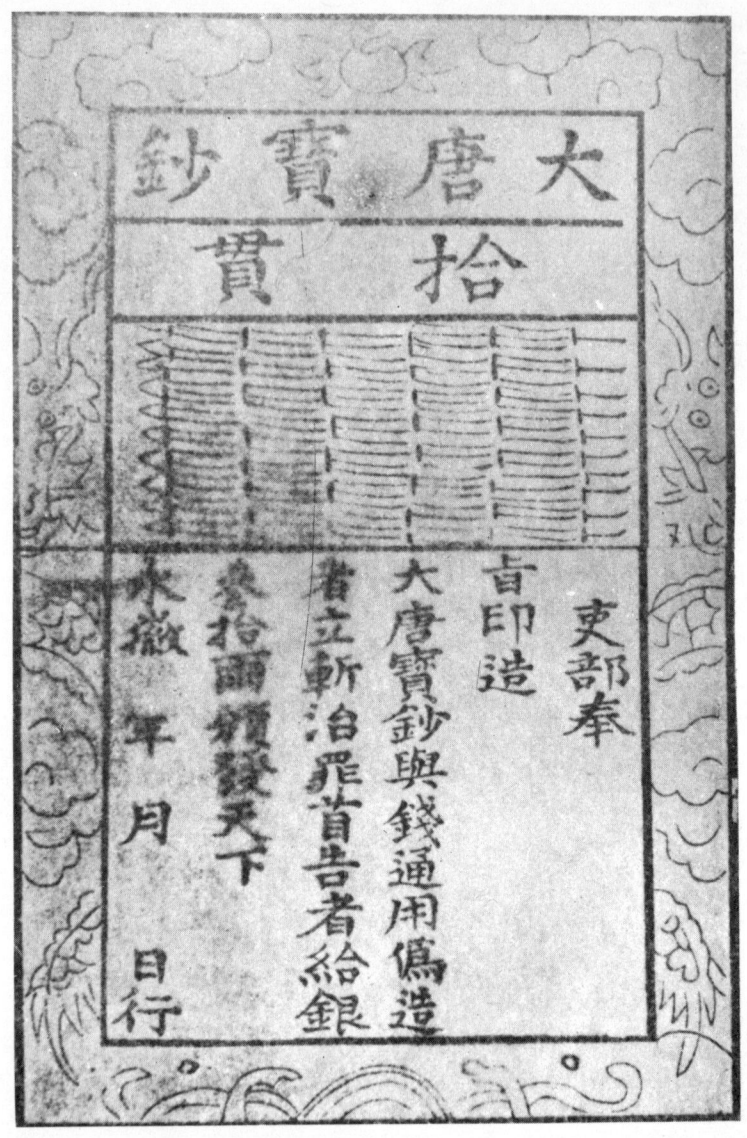

10 Kwan note of the T'ang Dynasty AD 650

8 the orient

china

It was not until comparatively recent years that collectors began to take an interest in paper money and, because of this, its origin remains a mystery. The student knows beyond doubt that paper money was introduced by the Chinese and that there was no possibility of having paper money proper before circa 200 AD, for it was not until then that paper was invented.

But the forerunner of paper money, leather, was in use in China before the birth of Christ. A well-recorded instance is that of Emperor Wu Ti of the Western Han dynasty who made an issue of hide money in 119 BC. White deer were slaughtered for the purpose and their hides cut into squares of one foot, ornamented with floral designs, and marked for various high denominations. The reason for the issue is somewhat obscure. Some authorities say that the emperor was running short of money and issued the money to tribute-visiting war-lords. It was the custom for war-lords to pay tribute annually to the emperor and on this occasion it would appear that the tribute was decided for them, each being presented with the hide money and being required to pay for it in cash. The alternative was beheading, so the emperor's treasury was replenished.

Other authorities, however, contend that his bodyguard of Manchurian mercenaries revolted as they had not been paid and the white deer hide money was quickly manufactured for their pay. In view of the high denominations either the soldiers had not been paid for a long time or they were the highest paid soldiers in the world!

The first recorded use of paper money as such is an issue made between 650 and 655 AD by Emperor Yung Hue of the Tang dynasty. While no examples of this paper money have come to light, these notes are actually illustrated in an early numismatic work and fully described. Beyond doubt paper money circulated in 800 AD and, it is believed, examples have been preserved in the Peking museum. But this was not fiat money as it was a government draft instructing provinces to exchange the draft for bronze money. They were negotiable bills and were termed 'fei-chien' which, roughly translated, means 'flying money'

This money was extremely popular. Wealthy merchants travelling in the vast wastes of China had found the heavy bronze coinage a burden. Wagons could only crawl along under the weight of the heavy coinage and the whole convoy was tempting bait to marauding bandits who abounded in the wild countryside. The introduction of fei-chein meant that fast riders could travel across country in much less danger.

With the Sung dynasty came paper money proper, redeemable against cash. Initiated by the government around 1000 AD, the issue was soon in trouble owing to the almost continual warfare, and it was not long before its value depreciated. It is interesting to note that in that year no less than 16 private banks had been given authority to issue their own notes in the Szechuan Province alone. The Sung government money, djiau-dze (exchangeable money) was changed to quei-dze (citadel money), but this too was soon in trouble and was responsible in some degree for the downfall of the Sung dynasty itself.

There is no doubt that China made a determined effort to control its note issues, for as early as 1023 a special bureau, Yih Chu Chiao Tzu Wu, was formed to supervise the issue of Chiao Tzu paper money being issued by private banks – and later taken over by the government.

Early paper money did not circulate indefinitely and had a life of three years. Later it became the practice to replace worn paper money with new for a small charge by the government.

By 1161 paper money to the value of 41 million kuan (1 kuan

equalled 1000 cash) was in circulation. Whereas in the West gold and silver have always been more highly valued than paper, the Chinese emperors gave their paper money the aura of invincibility and proclaimed that it was much more desirable than cash and should be treated so. To ensure circulation a proportion of government taxes had to be paid in paper money instead of coin.

The Mongols (Yuan dynasty, 1260–1368 AD) swept into China under the famous Kublai Khan and quickly established their rule over part of China. They soon saw the advantages of paper money and were quick to follow the Sung dynasty rulers in issuing paper money. For a time the Mongol notes were successful as, for some twenty years, they were backed by a silver system. But the Mongols were essentially conquerors and by now their commitments to hold land they had taken by the sword were becoming enormous.

They now did something which was soon to become commonplace throughout the world. Unable to pay their soldiers, they simply resorted to the printing press and issued military paper money which had no backing in silver or bronze. By 1358 AD their paper money was worthless and the mighty Mongols were at the same time obliged to relinquish their hold on China.

A few of these early notes are in existence in the national museums of China itself but not one is in the possession of private collectors.

It is from this era, however, that we have our first full descriptions of paper money. Marco Polo brought back a racy description of the 'means whereby the Great Khan may have, and in fact has, more treasure than all the Kings of the World'. If Marco were disbelieved there were five other well-known European travellers and writers from the thirteenth to the fifteenth century who independently gave accounts of the Chinese paper money system: William de Rubruquis, Roger Bacon, Hayton, Pegollotti and Josafat Barbara. Arabic writers also gave accounts, particularly Ibn Batuta (1348) and Ahmed Shibab Eddi (1338).

Marco Polo observed: 'They are so light that ten bezants worth does not weigh one golden bezant . . . and with this paper money the merchants can buy what they like anywhere over the Empire whilst it is also vastly lighter to carry about on their journeys'.

The Ming dynasty which came to power in 1368 followed the Mongols in issuing paper money and it is notable that in essence the production of paper money was the same from the beginning. Indeed Marco Polo's description of the notes would apply equally to Ming paper money. They were not exactly handy little things, as they measured 9 inches by 13 inches and were made from the bark of mulberry trees – known for their endurance – and printed from wooden blocks. These imperial banknotes were issued by the Emperor T'Aitsu Hung Wa Ming, founder of the dynasty, and are probably the first examples of paper money of the world obtainable by collectors.

Coloured dark slate, the inscription, in Chinese characters, at the top of the note reads: 'Government of Ming Empire'. The borders are attractively designed with arabesque style and dragons. In the centre are two panels. The top panel reads: 'One Kwan' over a pictorial illustration of piles of coins. On the side of the panel is a square seal which somewhat hopefully can be translated 'Government Note of the Ming Empire circulating for Ever and Ever'.

It is clear that by this time the Chinese had suffered from forgery for the notes contain a statement in the second panel which reads: 'The Imperial Board of Revenue, having memorialized the Throne, has received the Imperial sanction for the issue of Government notes of the Ming Empire to circulate on the same footing as standard cash. To counterfeit is death. The informant will receive 250 taels in silver and in addition the entire property of the criminal.'

Later the Chinese adopted the unusual and highly successful practice of not executing forgers but setting them to work to make government notes.

Early in the Ming dynasty paper money was declared the only legal tender and it became a serious offence to transact business in gold or silver.

These notes first came to light when British soldiers were looting in Peking during the Boxer Rebellion. Some men knocked down a statue of the Buddha and found a pile of Ming notes deposited in the base. They had been put there in the same manner that Western nations place coins etc. under foundation stones.

110

Ming Dynasty note, *c.* 1368

When the first note came up for sale in 1900 it fetched $3,600. However, as more came to light the price quickly dropped to a mere $25. Today they are among the great rarities of the world, representing the first paper money still in existence, and fetch well over £300 each. It is interesting to reflect that they were in use one hundred years before the discovery of America.

Inflation soon invalidated the Ming paper money and by 1436 the government discontinued the issues and resorted to cash. For 200 years no official paper money circulated in China and then, with the advent of the Ta Ching dynasty in 1644, a paper issue was attempted in 1651 known as Kuan Chao. The issue never took root and ten years later the Manchus were obliged to withdraw it altogether.

Paper money did not appear in China again, as far as we know, until the T'ai P'ing Rebellion of 1854-9. Led by a school-teacher who felt he had been called upon by God to stop the worship of idols, societies were formed in the provinces of Kwangtung and Kwangsi. An adventurer, Chu Chiu-t'ao, then seized a Kwangsi city on their behalf, although in so doing he was captured and executed. The insurgents, however, moved to Hunan and down the Yangtze where they took Nanking and ruled for a decade. In desperate straits for revenue, the Imperial Government issued Hsien Feng notes and at the same time introduced internal transit taxes on commerce and maritime customs. The notes ranged from 500 to 100,000 cash and there was one issue for 50 taels. But within a very short time of their issue they depreciated to a mere three per cent of face value.

When next paper money made its appearance in any strength, at around the turn of the century, it took on a Western look, and collectors take the Tai Ping Rebellion as the dividing line between early Chinese paper money and modern Chinese paper money.

It is with the modern issues that the collector really comes into his own. Here it is feasible for a collector of fairly limited means to compile a collection of some 2,000 different notes of this period of China. There are many thousands of different notes, but a great many are rare, and almost yearly notes turn up which hitherto were unknown to collectors.

Apart from the attraction that China first used paper money, China's popularity among collectors is due to the elaborate and intricate designs of their modern notes combined with the history that lies behind their issue.

For a long time the government took no real interest in paper issues, their past history being one of failure, and these were therefore left to the war-lords. The war-lords were engaged in almost continual internecine warfare, and some of them ruled over very small territories while others were so powerful that the main government would have been hard put to lay down the law. Colourful paper money was issued in abundance and often without any real backing. Indeed one war-lord openly boasted that he would start a bank without any capital – Feng Yu-hsiang (Bank of the Northwest) – and he chose a dynamited railway station as the design for the notes. They circulated in Fengchen at the point of the bayonet.

When a war-lord found himself in difficulty with his bank notes he would often simply close the bank – perhaps even execute the luckless bank-manager as an appeasement to the people – and open up again under a different name with a different design. Naturally collectors have a lot of fun unravelling the stories that lie behind these issues.

Sound banking with note-issues that were acceptable to the people came basically from foreign banks which set up branches in China. In fact the first foreign bank, a British one, opened for business even before the Tai Ping Rebellion. This was the Bank of Western India which opened a branch in Hong Kong after the Sino-British Opium War of 1842. It changed its name to the Oriental Bank and was soon well established. Next came the Commercial Bank of India which started a branch in Canton in 1851 and another in Shanghai in 1855.

Other banks followed quickly and it is possible to form a specialised collection of the note-issues of foreign banks in China.

Russia, which lent money to China to ransom the Liao Tun Peninsula from Japan, was allowed to open the Russo-Chinese Bank just after the first Sino-Japanese War. The United States also had banks operating in China, the International Banking Corporation – 1902 – and the Pao Hsin Yin Hang of 1864.

Germany, France, Belgium and Holland all circulated special paper money for use in China.

Chinese revolutionary government note

At the turn of the century the Chinese Government did dabble in the banking world with the Ta Ching Treasury Bank, started in 1904, and the Bank of Communications, in 1907. They took the unusual step of allowing the public to buy shares in the banks, no doubt in the hope of gaining their trust. Banks like the Commercial Bank of China which were to be taken over by the nation started even earlier (1897), but under the name of the Imperial Bank of China.

But these banks did not operate on modern lines and it was not until the advent of Dr Sun Yat Sen that anything like banking as understood in the West was introduced in China. Sun Yat Sen's Confederacy Society of China, which started in Japan in 1905, put the torch to revolutionary feeling and ousted the Ch'ing dynasty.

Sun Yat Sen's first issue of notes is keenly sought after by collectors. When the Ch'ing government asked Japan to arrest him and return him to China for execution the Japanese warned him and he escaped to Vietnam. There he issued bonds to the value of 10,000 Vietnamese dollars. Headed 'The Chinese Revolutionary Government' they were issued on 1 January 1906. Various types were issued and some were smuggled into China proper and used by the revolutionary army under Commander Li Yuan Hung, who was later to become the third president of the Republic of China. In 1911 Sun Yat Sen made another issue of bonds from San

Bank of Communications notes usually have vignettes relating to transport and communications like this attractive reverse design of 1914

Francisco in high denominations, $1000, $100 and $10. These notes carry the signatures of Sun Yat Sen as prime minister and of Lee Kung Sh'ia, treasurer to the Chinese Revolutionary Army.

Such issues carried a pledge to redeem them in silver after the establishment of the Republic. True to its word, the Republic redeemed them after the fifth National meeting held in September 1935 and because of this the notes are extremely rare.

When Chiang Kai-Shek made his bid for power the main backing was an issue of paper money for the famous march to the North.

The currency reform of 1935 put China almost entirely on to a paper money system and for a time everything seemed successful. Then the Japanese invasion of 1937 brought a repetition of the inflation that China had seen so often before.

Collectors are sometimes confused by the different types of paper money used by the Chinese. The principle behind them was that once a type of note ceased to retain its value the government would resort to another. Hence we see custom gold units, officially started for paying custom duties, but soon circulating generally. Collectors find early issues for one and five units but, as inflation crept forward, the issues rose to 25,000, 50,000 and even 250,000 custom gold units. An attempt was made to stabilise the issues by dating them earlier. So we see notes issued in 1942 which are dated for the 1930s.

Once the custom gold units had got out of hand the Kuomintang government issued a new currency, on 19 August 1948 – the gold yuan. The population were told that no notes would be issued with a face value of over GY 100. But by 1949 denominations were reaching 50,000. They came to a halt when the Communist armies marched into Shanghai on 25 May of that year.

The Central Bank of China in Canton continued to act for the government but changed the currency; this time it was silver dollar certificates.

Another type of note in China which attracts specialists is the copper note. These are for small denominations and circulated extensively during the latter part of the nineteenth century and the beginning of the twentieth century. Often poorly printed, they were soon forged. Because of this some copper notes carried, in the English language, the Chinese idea of a warning to examine notes carefully: 'Not pay to-night'. It was intended to warn against accepting the note in poor light, and some notes, notably those of the Yu Hwa Bank, have the spelling wrong, reading: 'Not pay to Nioht'.

Some provinces banned copper notes, as did Kirin in 1921 when a grain merchant bought a large shipment and paid for it with his

Customs gold units and gold Yuan overprinted for military use

Top One of the many note-issues of foreign banks in China.
Bottom The Dragon design of China, *circa* 1938

own, hastily produced, copper notes. He then disappeared together with the merchandise.

The research specialist has plenty of scope in the field of copper notes and some authorities, particularly the late E. Kann, assert that there are probably more different copper note issues than general issues of China.

There is no better way to illustrate the history of China than through its paper issues. The fortunes of the Communist and Kuomintang parties are seen through their note issues.

Once Japan had gained a strong foothold in China its influence on paper money was considerable. Two gigantic banking organisations were set up, the Federal Reserve Bank of China and the

Reserve Bank of China. At first sight the early issues appear to be Chinese with no Japanese influence whatsoever and are even printed with English-language reverses. The Japanese quickly changed that, and so notes in English from Japanese controlled banks are very scarce today.

It happened that the Chinese engravers of the notes went to some extremes to let it be known that they did not like the Japanese, and various designs incorporate anti-Japanese propaganda. One particular note has on it, hidden in various parts of the scrollwork, the letters USAC which, it is said, stands for, United States Army Coming. At all events the engravers were in trouble for the issue and steps were taken to change it.

It is probable that a specialist collection of more than 30,000 Chinese notes could be formed, and that without much trouble a new collector could get together an informative and large collection. Few countries offer the interest and scope that is found in Chinese notes. It is interesting too, that most of China's notes were printed outside China by world-famous British and American banknote printing firms.

korea

Korea presents the paper money collector with a wealth of interest. First, dominated by Chinese influence, it issued mulberry-type paper money in the fourteenth century. Russian and Japanese attempts to dominate the territory at the turn of the nineteenth century left behind them paper money. Japanese influence was at its greatest during World War II and immediately afterwards American influence can be seen. Then came the Korean war with attempts to destroy the economy by flooding it with forged South Korean notes, and forcing North Korean notes on the public.

Paper money can be traced back to 1391 AD when the Chasom Chohwago was established to print mulberry paper money. The building burned down together with the stocks of printed paper money just before issue was due and it was not until 1401 that King Taejoing ordered paper money to be printed. Hemp cloth also circulated but was soon stopped.

In 1415 the minting of coin was suspended to enforce circulation of mulberry paper money. Under King Sejoing (1424) coins established themselves over paper money which was called in at the rate of one note for one coin (a Cho Son T'ong Bo).

Shortage of coins led to paper money becoming the standard currency again in 1445 but it died out when coins became readily available.

The first National Bank of Japan, Dai Ichi Ginko, opened branches in Pusan and Inchon following a customs tariff agreement with Korea and issued bills for the payment of customs duties in 1884. The merchants found them convenient and began using them in normal transactions.

A Russo-Korean Bank was established by Tsarist Russia at its Legation in Seoul and soon printed paper money. It was part of Russia's attempt to infiltrate into the Far East, a move which was noted by Japan and Britain to the extent of sending a fleet into the harbour and ensuring that anti-Russian party members gained power.

In 1902 the Japanese Government granted a concession to the Japanese bank in Korea to issue unregistered drafts payable at sight. It was an attempt to gain financial control. The pro-Russians in the Korean Government countered this move by placing inspectors at various ports with orders to prohibit the use of this money. But as the Japanese had taken care to back the notes with gold the public preferred them, and Japanese diplomats bargained with Korean officials to lift the ban on eight ports. In 1904 Japanese soldiers were stationed in Korea for the war against Tsarist Russia and the Japanese bank had no further trouble with its notes.

Indeed the Dai Ichi Ginko assumed the functions of the Central Bank in Korea and handled Treasury accounts until 1909 when the Bank of Korea was established. The agreement provided that the notes issued by Dai Ichi Ginko should be regarded as the issues of the Bank of Korea, which accepted responsibility for them: an unusual step considering that a foreign nation was involved. At the time 11,833,127 won notes were in circulation.

With the annexation of Korea by Japan in 1910 the bank was changed to the Central Bank of Chosen to be changed again the following year to the Bank of Chosen. As commerce grew and expanded the Bank of Chosen notes circulated in the Kwantung province and South Manchuria, territory formerly under the Yokohama Specie Bank in Japan, and by 1917 the Bank of Chosen enjoyed wide circulation. Once Japan entered into a full-scale war with China, Bank of Chosen notes were permitted throughout Japanese-dominated China.

Korea was officially liberated on 15 August 1945 and to avoid financial catastrophe Bank of Chosen notes were allowed to continue as the only legal tender notes. Nippon Ginko notes and Japanese National Treasury bonds were cancelled. Under American control and influence the whole structure was investigated and the new Bank of Korea was inaugurated on 12 June 1950. Hardly had it started business than the Korean War broke out and the government was forced to move to Pusan, the bank's headquarters going with it. New notes were issued. The North Korean Peoples' Bank made its notes circulate in occupied areas of South Korea by force and forged 1,000 won notes of the Bank of Korea (they were not actually issued) and 100 won notes to destroy the economy in the South.

The effect was enough to oblige the government, on 14 February 1953, to issue an urgent presidential decree (no. 13) invalidating the 'won' and replacing it with the 'Hwan' notes.

Yet another upheaval came in 1960 when the student revolution overthrew the Syngman Rhee administration. New notes were printed and a portrait of King Sejong the Great replaced the President. In 1962 a third currency reform was carried out to avoid inflation, and these notes were still current in 1970. Issues of 1, 5, 10, 50, 100 and 500 won were made by Thomas De La Rue and later most denominations by the Korean Government Printing Agency. Early Korean printed notes were offset and poor quality in comparison with those of De La Rue.

tibet

The paper money of Tibet has a particular interest to collectors because its method of manufacture remained the same until the recent Chinese occupation.

Clearly the Tibetans learned the art of paper making from the Chinese, and as the methods are the same as those used in ancient

Tibetan note made by monks

Cathay it is to be assumed that Tibetan paper money circulated at or around that time.

Lama monks first fashioned wooden blocks of birchwood and then laboriously carved the script letters into the wood.

For printing ink they used a solution made by burning yak dung and mixing it with various types of earth to produce colours. Strong hand-made native paper, complete with watermark, was used, and lastly the seals were added. The two sides of the note were then pasted together to form a single note and the number was painted on by hand.

This was the method used by the ancient Chinese in the thirteenth century. The modern range of paper money started with the previous cycle, 1867–1927, (in the Tibetan calendar beginning in 1658). Buddhist symbols and scenes form the designs.

japan

Paper money first made its appearance in Japan at the Ka Na Kai-Ko port – now the Ginza of Tokyo. Although an issue of notes is known in the first year of Kenbu of Emperor Daigo, 1334 AD, paper money did not circulate widely until the eighteenth century.

121

Hansatsu 'bookmark' issues of Japan, AD 1700

Many of these early notes, affectionately called 'bookmark money' by collectors because of their resemblance to bookmarks in shape, need further research. Attractive, they were produced by many organisations and they marked the beginning of the end of the famous 'warrior class' of Japan. As in other parts of the world, the wealth of the merchants gradually gave them more power than the warriors who, like British noblemen of medieval times, regarded business as a sordid and contemptible occupation. But now they had need to compete with the merchants and in a last desperate effort to preserve their authority issued their own paper money.

At different times the Japanese notes were known as Kuni-Satsu, Hansatsu, Shisatsu, Kinsatsu, Komesatsu, Kasatsu, and Okura Da Kan Sho (Treasury Convertible Bill). Some of these notes still circulated at the turn of the nineteenth century.

Because of their long circulation counterfeiting became a

serious threat and in 1811 the old notes were replaced by new paper money carefully printed in Germany in order to defeat counterfeiters.

Japan also had local money exchange shops and these institutions issued their own paper money known as Kin Ken (gold note), Gin Ken (silver note), Sen Ken (copper note) and Yo Gin Ken (New Mexican silver dollar).

The currency was a yen made up of 100 sen. During the Meiji reign much of the paper money became unredeemable and in the fourteenth year of the reign the currency was called in at the rate of $1 yo gin ken to 81 sen. In the thirtieth year of Jeiji laws were made for the first time which restricted the amount of issues any financial institution could make. A reserve fund was started to ensure that notes would be redeemed. This had the effect of putting the Japanese economy on a firm foundation.

One of the most interesting and inexpensive series of notes open to collectors today is that of the Japanese Occupation notes. These are colourful and well-prepared issues in most cases, being part of the carefully laid plans to establish a Co-Prosperity Sphere for Greater East Asia. Some of the areas co-operated with the scheme to a greater degree than they would now like to recall but most areas soon found that the Asian Japanese overlord was no better, and indeed usually much worse, than the European overlords of pre-war days.

When the occupation paper money first found its way to the United States it fetched high prices as, at that time, collectors did not know the true rarity. Some of the notes are rare but the great majority are worth only a shilling or two each.

Collectors can identify the areas notes were used in by the code letters on them.

P	= Philippines	B	= Burma
M	= Malaya	O	= Oceania
S	= (Sumatra), Dutch East Indies		

The Philippines came under attack at the same time as Pearl Harbour and in December 1941 Japanese troops made a series of seaborne invasions. Manila fell on 2 January 1942 and the famous drive on Bataan followed. After that only guerillas continued resistance and they issued their own paper money. Natives were afraid to accept guerilla money because Japanese patrols coming to their village would regard possession of guerilla currency as a capital offence.

First issues of Philippines show the Rizal monument or a banana grove. Then a puppet regime was set up in the Philippines under Dr José P. Laurel and new notes were issued.

Thousand peso notes were printed in Baguio by Japanese authorities who now experienced the printing difficulties which had beset the guerillas for so long because American troops had returned and were surrounding the area. They are testimony to the high inflation and the fact that some Japanese officials were beginning to 'salt away' a few high notes just in case the conquering Allies decided to redeem the circulating money. Purple ink was used and appears to be duplicator or hectograph ink; it soaked through to the back of the notes.

Many occupation notes of the Philippines will be found with two quarter-inch circular punched holes in them. This was done by the American Red Cross and the notes then distributed as souvenirs.

An interesting propaganda note can be found. The genuine Philippine occupation notes were overprinted by American forces in large capitals 'The Co-Prosperity Sphere: What is it worth?'

A last-minute attempt by the Japanese to get their notes accepted once the Americans had landed was made by an issue of 'The Republic of the Philippines' picturing José Rizal, the great patriot. But they were too late and did not go into circulation.

General MacArthur set up his headquarters in the Trade and Commerce Building, Juan Luna Street, Manila, and the Wilson Building next door was found to contain the supply depot for occupation notes of all Japanese-occupied territories. Despite heavily armed guards being immediately put round the depot, vaults were blasted open and notes of an unknown quantity stolen. The remainder, vast stocks, were burned at the service entrance to the building.

Malaya notes are particularly colourful and attractive and include the 10 dollar banana note – most Japanese occupation money became contemptuously referred to as 'banana money'

$1000 Japanese Occupation note of Malaya

implying it was useless. But when these Malayan notes (identified only by the code letter M) first came into the hands of Americans it was thought they had been prepared for the invasion of the United States. It was not generally appreciated that 'dollars' were the currency of Malaya. Consequently they fetched high prices until the quantities available and their true history became known. Complete sets from the 1 cent to 1000 dollars even now only fetch a pound or two. The ten dollar note was copied by the Americans and issued as a propaganda note with the text on the reverse in the three languages spoken in Malaya.

The 'S' notes for Dutch East Indies were printed in the Dutch language and the Japanese were able to make use of imprisoned native intellectuals who even before the war had been advocating an independent Indonesia. Among them was Dr Sukarno (later president of Indonesia). The Japanese were thus able to count on the friendship of the puppet regime they set up and encouraged them to actively dislike their former overlords. At the end of the war the Japanese had done the job so well that Indonesia was born.

Most of the area was primitive except for Sumatra and Java where there was a comparatively high degree of literacy.

In Java the Japanese prohibited the use of Dutch in 1943 when the native regime took over under the Japanese influence. Notes were then printed in the native tongue, 'Pemerintah Dai Nippon' for 'the Japanese Government'. The word 'Roepiah' replaced

'Gulden' (the Dutch gilders) and the last issues show a native dancer on the obverse and Buddha on the reverse, thus becoming distinctive from all other Japanese occupation-type paper money.

The 'B' notes of Burma are common and for much of the war British troops slogged their way through the jungles occasionally capturing quantities of these issues. Taking advantage of the fact that the Burmese did not particularly care for the British and still less for the Chinese, the Japanese set up a puppet government under Dr Ba Maw in 1943, which issued distinctive paper money with a peacock design overprinted in Burmese 'Burma State'.

While at first many Burmese in military service deserted to the Japanese side they soon decided that the British were the lesser of two evils and the puppet regime did not enjoy the power the Japanese had anticipated.

The scarcest general issue of Japanese occupation money is that of Oceania, code letter 'O', for the British possessions of South Pacific islands like New Guinea, the Solomons and the Gilbert Islands. The notes are unusual in that they are the only denominations printed by the Japanese in sterling currency, $\frac{1}{2}$ shilling, shilling, ten shillings and one pound. They depict an island palm tree view. Australians and Allied forces disputed the jungle territory continuously – it was imperative not to allow the area to be used as a jumping-off stage for the invasion of Australia and the notes never enjoyed the circulation of the other Japanese-occupied territories.

Combat troops returning to Australia for a rest period from New Guinea took home some of these notes as early as 1943 and the demand for them was such that they were copied and, with the word Replica on them, sold to the public. Ironically, the Replica notes are now rarer than the originals!

Japan also controlled many paper money issues in parts of China – which are dealt with in the Chinese section. In Thailand they had overall control by the presence of their troops but the Siamese (whose puppet Japanese government declared war on Great Britain in 1942 – an act repudiated by the nation at the conclusion of hostilities) issued their own wartime paper money, as did Indo-China, occupied by Japanese troops on the authority of the Vichy French Government.

126

9 africa

The continent of Africa is vast and its paper issues extremely colourful and sometimes bizarre. Many recent political upheavals have left their mark on paper money. Tshombe and others have had their faces reproduced on paper money during their short terms of power.

With over 11,262,000 square miles and 250,000,000 people it is not surprising that a considerable amount of paper money exists. Little is known about many of these nations but South Africa has a long history of paper issues and is dealt with here at length. For the rest of Africa, new collectors will find an absorbing pastime collecting notes of the newly independent and colonial states.

south africa

The introduction of paper money in South Africa came about primarily through the war between Great Britain and the Netherlands. Dutch coin was in short supply and for some time many types of foreign coins had been used. In 1872 – a year after the outbreak of war – the situation was so critical, owing to the hoarding of gold and silver, that rix-dollar notes were issued to make up the deficiency of money.

Incredibly enough, there was no printing press in South Africa, so these first notes had to be hand-written and their seal of authority was the Dutch Government fiscal hand-stamp. It was intended to withdraw them as soon as new coin was made available and while this was achieved with the first issue it soon became necessary for more issues to be made.

127

They were easy to forge and issues were changed frequently to confound the forgers. By 1790 there was only about £500 worth of metal money in the Cape and paper money was established. With the first British occupation the rix-dollar paper money had depreciated by a quarter and there were some $1\frac{1}{4}$ million dollars in circulation. The British put some silver and gold into circulation by paying their troops with it, but this money disappeared quickly and as the position deteriorated the authorities granted permission for merchants to issue their own 'good-fors' as a way of providing small change. In 1803 when the Cape was made part of the Batavian Republic notes were printed and in January 1804 all existing paper money was called in for replacement by printed card money and stamped with seal of the Batavian Republic.

The second British occupation saw some two million rix-dollars circulating in paper money and in 1810 the notes were radically changed by having a new stamp impression of Britannia added, supplied by Messrs Halfhide Barnes and Co., of London.

The currency of Great Britain replaced Cape money in 1831 and all rix-dollars were called in, being replaced by promissory notes of £1, £5, £10, £20, £50 and £100.

The Lombard Bank was the first bank set up in the Cape, and was a state bank. The first private bank was that of Mr J. B. Ebden who, although he originally applied in 1825, did not get permission until 1837. Governor Lord Charles Somerset issued a decree that no banknotes for less than 50 rix-dollars (equivalent to £3. 15s.) were to be issued and, until 1891 all notes were for denominations of £4 (smaller denominations exist, but were never actually issued).

As South Africa prospered so more banks made their appearance and the following issued paper money in their own names:

Cape of Good Hope Bank
Bank of South Africa
South African Bank
Eastern Province Bank
Colonial Bank
Port Elizabeth Bank
Frontier Commercial and Agricultural Bank

Western Province Bank
Union Bank
Graaff-Reinet Bank
Worcester Commercial Bank
Paarl Bank
Swellendam Bank
Commercial Bank of Port Elizabeth
Cape Commercial Bank
South African Central Bank
Beaufort Bank
Stellenbosch Bank
Wellington Bank
Uitenhage Bank
Cradock Union Bank
British Kaffrarian Bank
Queenstown Bank
Somerset East Bank
George Divisional Bank
Fort Beaufort and Victoria Bank
Caledon Agricultural Bank
Montagu Bank
Colesburg Bank
Albert Bank
Malmesbury Agricultural and Commercial Bank
Kaffrarian Colonial Bank
Agricultural Bank of Queenstown
Stellenbosch District Bank
National Bank of the S. A. R.
London and South African Bank
Standard Bank of British South Africa
Oriental Bank Corporation
Bank of Africa
African Banking Corporation

Most of these were well established before 1863 but by 1893 only four were still operating:

A few large private business houses also issued notes, principally Barry and Nephews, Swellendam, in 1850; Namaqua Mining

Unissued Swellandan note by Barry and Nephews

Company, in 1850; Mosenthal Brothers, Cape Town, between 1854 and 1860; and Phillips and King of Namaqualand, also between 1854 and 1860.

From 1891 the Bank Act required all banks to deposit securities equal to the note issues.

Natal had no official issues of paper money, but nine private banks issued their own banknotes.

Only three banks were established in the Orange Free State by local interests, though branches were opened by some Cape banks. The first notes were those of the Bloemfontein Bank, 1862-77. As none of these banknotes were for less than £1 and coin was scarce, good-fors were issued frequently by business firms and individuals.

The South African Republic (Transvaal) suffered from a shortage of money as well and the government issued 'mandaten' (Treasury bills) in 1857. Although the Cape rix-dollar notes had ceased to be legal tender in the Cape they were still used in the Transvaal and a further issue was now made by the South African Republic in 1865 (five and ten rix-dollar notes carrying six per cent interest). In 1866 when the pound sterling was adopted the second issue of paper money was made and for the first time the Republic's coat of arms, as approved by the Volksraad in 1857

130

featured on the notes. More issues were made in 1867 and 1868, all printed locally on paper except for small-denomination good-fors which were on cardboard. An issue was printed in England and released in 1871 – the last regular issue of the Republic.

The difficulty in getting the people to accept paper money led to the president and vice-president of the Republic personally hand-signing these notes to show their authenticity.

A number of banks issued notes, and the most famous of these was the De Nederlandsche Bank en Crediet-Vereeniging voor Zuid-Africka Bpkt, the forerunner of the present Netherlands Bank of South Africa.

In 1890 a consortium of German, Dutch and British interests obtained a banking concession and established the De Nationale Bank der Zuid-Afrikaansche Republiek Bpkt in 1891 at Pretoria. It acted as banker to the government, which undertook not to accept the notes of other banks in any of its departments. Beautiful notes were produced featuring a bust of President S. J. P. Kruger. The bank prospered and by 1900 had thirty-three branches.

One of the most fascinating series of paper money is that issued during the Boer War when both sides used paper money under extreme emergencies. Shortly before hostilities Kruger seized all the gold in the banks, with which the government purchased war material. By 1900 money was so short that it was decided to issue paper money and notes were issued at Pretoria, dated 28 May 1900, for £1, £5, £10, £20, £50, and £100.

When British forces occupied Pretoria a new issue of notes was made at Pietersburg dated 1 February 1901, 1 March 1901, and 1 April 1901 for identical denominations. The Boers fled on horse-back with the printing press used for these notes when British troops entered Pietersburg. British troops overran the area – and some of these notes can be found with overstamp 'Captured and Cancelled'. Early in 1902 the Boers made their final issues of paper money dated 1 March 1902, 1 April 1902 and 1 May 1902 with the words, 'Te Velde' indicating that these were issued 'in the field'. These were for £1, £5, and £10 only and were issued at Pilgrim's Rest. The last issue was made on white ruled paper of the kind used in school note-books.

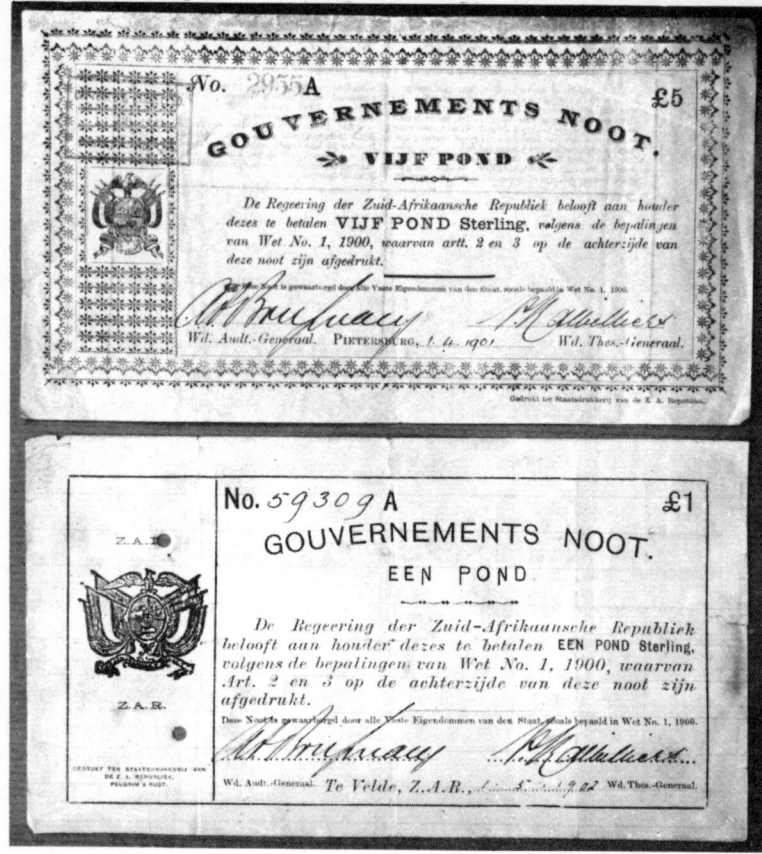

Kruger notes of the Boer War

British emergency notes issued during the Boer War are keenly sought-after items, particularly those of the siege of Mafeking which lasted for 217 days. Colonel Baden-Powell, later to become the founder of the Boy Scouts, issued these notes under his authority.

Colonel Baden-Powell helped produce these notes and drew on copper the first design for the £1 note – which depicted a man with a field gun and another with a Maxim gun. The design was then etched with acid. But printing presented insurmountable problems, and even when a mangle was used it was found that sufficient pressure could not be obtained to print the notes clearly.

Mr E. C. Ross pictured manufacturing the Mafeking siege notes and a picture of the bank

The 10s note issued during the siege. Only a few thousand exist

The local watchmaker, Mr C. Riesle, then made a woodcut from the design, using a croquet mallet cut in half for the block, but even this failed to give satisfactory results, though later it was used, with slight modifications, for the ten shilling note (green).

Colonel Baden-Powell now designed a completely different £1 note with the Union Jack defiantly flying over the defenders, a main part of the design being 'The Wolf' – a gun made entirely from bits and pieces and with British ingenuity which was to surprise the Boers. It was named 'The Wolf' after Baden-Powell. For a long time the Africans had nicknamed him 'The Wolf that never sleeps'.

German East Africa note, 1905

Printed photographically by the ferro-prussiate process by Mr E. C. Ross, they were produced at the rate of twenty a day in a 'dug-out' bank. The notes were printed in blue.

Two main types of the ten shilling note exist, one printed: 'Issued by authority of Col. R. S. S. Baden-Powell, Commaning Frontier Forces'. The subsequent issue had this corrected to 'Commanding'. Small denomination notes of 1s., 2s., and 3s. were also printed, and for these white 'Croxley' writing paper was used.

Notes were signed by the Chief Paymaster, Captain Greener, and the £1 and 10s. notes also carried the signature of Mr. R. Urry, Manager of the Standard Bank. The Bechuanaland Protectorate embossed penny revenue stamp was applied to notes to make them valid.

Sergeant-Major Jollie's native assistant, Jim Phuthego, stole some notes from the store but was caught because they did not bear the embossed stamp or signatures – he received twenty lashes and three months' hard labour.

Research by Scout Commissioner J. P. Ineson has revealed that these notes are scarcer than many collectors thought. Only 683 £1 notes were issued, 7,000 10s. notes and £1,045 worth of 1s., 2s., and 3s. notes. More were in fact printed at a later date but the siege was lifted and they were not issued. Strangely enough, by

1907 only £522 worth of these notes had been redeemed and it is interesting to note that even during the siege people were collecting souvenirs (siege postage stamps were offered for sale in the *Mafeking Mail* before the siege was over!).

Notes were also issued under emergency conditions at Koffiefontein and Upington. At Upington notes were issued to the Border Scouts on green poplin.

Prisoner of War camp notes were issued for Green Point and Simonstown. The Commandant of Green Point autographed some of the notes – ironically, his name was 'J. Money'. Other notes are known headed 'British Military Authority' and it is believed that these were used in various parts of the territory.

Modern paper money of South Africa is very colourful and in 1961 a change was made to the rand when South Africa went decimal.

german east africa

During the early German administration of German East Africa there was a shortage of coin, and local promissory notes, credit notes and Post Office notes were issued. Then, in 1905, the German East Africa Bank was formed at Dar-es-Salaam and issued an attractive set of notes of 5, 10, 50 and 100 rupies.

War between Britain and Germany resulted in an issue of interim notes for 20 rupies in March 1915, and later of other denominations – 1, 5, 10, 50 and 200 rupies. They were roughly produced and the Germans did not expect them to be needed for long. But three years later the war was still on and the German situation had worsened. Another issue of interim notes appeared, even more primitive than the first. These 'Bush notes' were printed by a rubber printing set and hand-signed. The last issue was made in 1917.

kenya (republic of)

The Republic of Kenya issued its first banknotes on 14 September 1966. They comprised 5, 10, 20, 50 and 100 shilling notes. A portrait of the President of Kenya and the nation's coat of arms appear on all obverses. Reverse designs show girls picking crops; the £1 shows a freight train carrying logs.

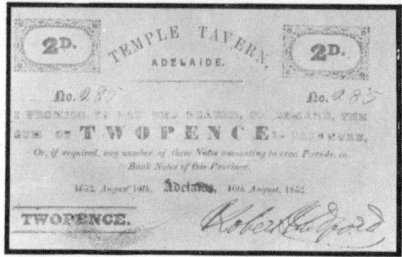

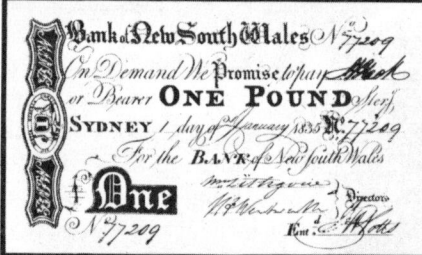

Various types of Australian
paper money all of which
are extremely rare today

10 australia and the pacific

Australia started its civilised history as a penal colony (the first fleet arrived in 1788) and the British Government paid no attention to the needs of the first settlement in Sydney Cove, leaving its inmates to look after themselves. This they did with an extraordinary assortment of paper money as well as whatever coins they could acquire, regardless of their country of origin.

Official Commissariat Store receipts for meat and grain were among the more acceptable items of paper money in the early days and military paymasters issued notes for purchases. As merchants developed their businesses they too issued 'promises to pay' notes in Sydney and Hobart. These are all extremely rare. They circulated – usually well below par, owing to forgery – until they crumbled to pieces.

Governor Macquarie was the first official to attempt seriously to put Australia's money affairs in order. He imported £10,000 worth of Spanish dollars and by removing the centres created two well-known numismatic items, the 'holey dollar' and the 'dump'. This action was not enough to stop the increasing number of private notes and the Governor authorised the Bank of New South Wales which opened in 1817 and was soon circulating some £12,000 worth of notes.

Early notes were in dollars but by 1829 the British Government enforced the sterling currency system on Australia. With the first big Australian boom some twenty banks began issuing notes, many of them with their headquarters in London. The depression of the 1840s caused many banks to disappear, but with the gold era that followed and the rush of people emigrating to Australia to seek their fortune, banking became established on a firm footing.

The oldest known example of Australian paper money is the Garnham Blaxcell £1 note of 1814. He, with other business men, agreed to build Sydney Hospital as part of a deal to import 60,000 gallons of rum, and he issued notes in payment of duties on his imports. His notes circulated in Sydney in defiance of Macquarie's order that duties must be paid in sterling, Spanish dollars or Commissariat bills.

Among the more interesting trader's notes are those of Ellis, Read and Company who issued £1 notes in Burketown in 1866. Operating in the outback, their notes were redeemable for cash in the big towns and were called 'shinplasters' because shearers would tuck them into their boots for safety until they reached the big towns. Some traders would deliberately treat shinplasters with flour and water so that they crumbled away before they could be presented for payment.

In 1966 Australia went decimal and notes were issued showing famous Australian people.

fanning island

An important relay station for the cable between Vancouver BC, Canada and Australia until June 1963, tiny Fanning Island is now part of the Gilbert and Ellice Islands. In 1939 it had a population of 740.

Japanese control of the seas made emergency money a necessity and Mr R. G. Garrett caused £1 notes to be printed in Hawaii for the island, headed: 'Fanning Island Plantations Ltd' – Fanning Island – One £ Pound, Australian Currency.

They were issued late in 1943. At the end of the war the notes were cancelled by cutting them in half, but they were then used as admission tickets to the cinema by copra plantation workers. The halves have 1s. and 2s. written on them in blue or red pencil.

Other Pacific islands made emergency issues. Fiji had to issue a note for one penny because soldiers took all the coins as souvenirs.

appendix: muslim dating

The new collector will come across various notes of Arabic nations with dates which appear to be medieval. They are not, and are different because they follow different calendars.

Western collectors can convert into the Western Gregorian calendar by subtracting three per cent from the Muslim date and adding 622. This gives an approximate conversion; a more accurate conversion can be obtained by multiplying the Muslim year by 0·970224, adding 621·5774 to the result and multiplying the decimal remainder by 365. This gives the year by the Gregorian calendar, correct to the day of its commencement.

The dates on Turkish notes can be converted to our dating system by adding 584.

bibliography

Bank of Canada, *The Story of Canada's Currency*.

Bank of Korea, *The Money of Korea*.

Berzins, E. and Musser, D. L., *Paper Money of the Baltic States, Latvia, Estonia and Lithuania*.

Charlton, J. E., *Canada and Newfoundland Paper Money, 1866-1935*.
Standard Catalogue of Canadian Coins, Tokens and Paper Money.

Chase, P. H., *Confederate Treasury Notes*.

Christoph, A. and Krause, C. *U.S. Postage and Fractional Currency*.

Collect British Banknotes. Stanley Gibbons Currency Ltd.

Criswell, Grover, *North American Currency*.
and Criswell, Clarence *Confederate and Southern State Currency*.

Davis, A. M., *Ancient Chinese Paper Money as described in a Chinese Work on Numismatics*.
Certain Old Chinese Bank Notes.

DeFanti, M., *Carta-Moneta Italiana (1866-1961)*

Denis, Ch., *Catalogue des Monnaies Emises sur la Territoire de la Russie (1914-25)*. (Tsarist and Revolutionary issues of Russia).

Donlon, W. P., *United States Small Size Paper Money*.

Elliot, J. A. Jr., *Canadian and Newfoundland Currency*.

Friedberg, R., *Paper Money of the United States*.

Gaytan, Carlos, *Billetes de Mexico*.

Gaytan, C. and Utberg, N. S. *The Paper Money of Mexico, 1822-1964*.

Giuseppi, J. *The Bank of England*.

Gould, M., *Hawaiian Coins, Tokens and Paper Money*.

Gould, M. and Higgie, L. W., *The Money of Puerto Rico*.

Howard, C. S., *Canadian Banks and Banknotes*.

Jablonski, Tadeusz, *Polski Pieniadz Papierowy* (Polish Paper Money).

Josset, C. R., *Money in Britain*.

Kadman, L., *Israel's Money*.

Kann, E., *History of Chinese Paper Money*, 3 Vols.

Karys, J. K., *Nepriklausomos Lietuvos Pinigai* (Currency of Independent Lithuania).

Keller, Dr Arnold, *Paper Money of the World. Part I, Modern issues of Europe*.

Das Papiergeld des Zweiten Weltkrieges. (The Paper money of World War II. 119 pages, 1953).

Das Papiergeld des Ersten Weltkriegs, Vol. I, Europa. (Paper money of the First World War, European).

Das Papiergeld des Ersten Weltkriegs, Vol. II. (Paper money of the First World War overseas).

Das Papiergeld des Deutschen Reiches von 1874-1945. (This is the standard reference work for German paper money).

Deutsche Kleingeldscheine 1916-1922. 3 Vols. 459 pages. *(Notgeld –* small emergency paper money).

Deutsche Grossgeldscheine, 1918-1921. (Large emergency paper money).

Das Notgeld der Deutschen Inflation. 1923. 8 vols.

Kugahara, *Catalogue of Military Currency of Japan*.

Kupa, Dr M., *Catalogue of Paper Money of the Yugoslavian States*.
Paper Money of Hungary.

Loeb, Dr W. M., *Catalog of Paper Money round the World*.

Limpert, F. A., *U.S. Postage Currency, 1862-1863, and Fractional Currency*.
United States National Banknotes, Original Series, First and Second Charter Periods.

Mackenzie, A. D., *The Bank of England Note*.

Miller, D. M., *Bank of England and Treasury Notes*.

Narbeth, C., *Coins and Currency*.
  Collecting Paper Money.

Newman, E. P., *The Early Paper Money of America*.

Ohasni Y., *Nippon Shihei Taikei Zukan. Illustrated Catalogue of Japanese Paper Money*. 371 pages. Standard reference work, with 10-page guide for English readers. Profusely illustrated.

Phillips, H., *Continental Paper Money*, 1866.

Pick, A., *Papiergeld*, (a 450-page book of paper money of the world including hundreds of illustrations, many in full colour).

Platbarzdis, I. A., *Sweden's Paper Money*.

Raymond, Wayte, *Standard Paper Money Catalogue of Colonial and Continental Currency*.

Reinfeld, F. A., *Story of Paper Money*.
  Simplified Guide to Collecting Mexican Paper Money.

Shafer, N., *A Guide Book of Modern United States Currency*.
  A Guide Book of Philippine Paper Money.

Skinner, D. H., *Rennik's Australian Coin and Banknote Guide*.

Slabaugh, A. R., *Confederate States Paper Money*.
  Japanese Invasion Money.
  Paper Money of the Mexican Revolution.
  Prisoner-of-War Moneys and Medals.

Societé d'Etude pour l'Histoire du Papier-Monnaie. *Les Billets de la Banque de France et du Tresore (1800-1952)*.

Sten, G. J., *Banknotes of the World*, Vol. 1. A – C

Sutherland, A., *Numismatic History of New Zealand*.

Swails, A. J., *Military Currency of World War II, U.S. and Allies*.

Taylor, H. C. and James, Somer, *The Guide Book of Canadian Coins, Paper Currency and Tokens*.

Thomson, W., *Dictionary of Banking*.

Tomlinson, G. W., *Australian Bank Notes, 1817-1963*.

Toy, R. S., *World War II Allied Military Currency*.

Toy, R. S. and Meyer, B., *Axis Military Currency World War II*.

Villefaigne, J. G., *Manuel Pratique du Change des Monnaies Etrangers*.

Werlich, R., *Catalog of U.S., Canadian and Confederate Currency*.

White, Benj., *The Currency of the Great War*.

index

143